FROM Incremental TO Exponential

FROM Incremental TO Exponential

VIVEK WADHWA AND ISMAIL AMLA

WITH ALEX SALKEVER

HARPER BUSINESS

An Imprint of HarperCollins *Publishers*

First published in 2020 by
Berrett-Koehler Publishers, Inc., USA

First published in India in 2020 by Harper Business
An imprint of HarperCollins *Publishers*

HarperCollins Publishers India, Cyber City, Building 10-A, Gurugram,
Haryana-122002, India

www.harpercollins.co.in

2 4 6 8 10 9 7 5 3 1

P-ISBN: 978-93-9032-710-2
E-ISBN: 978-93-9032-711-9

Typeset in 11/15 Adobe Garamond Pro at
Manipal Technologies Ltd, Manipal

Printed and bound at
MicroPrints India, New Delhi

MIX
Paper
FSC FSC® C218906

This product is made of FSC®-certified and other controlled material.

HarperCollins Publishers, Macken House, 39/40 Mayor Street
Upper, Dublin 1, D01 C9W8, Ireland

I dedicate this book to my late beloved wife, Tavinder. My soul mate, she continues to guide me in all earthly endeavors and to inspire my drive to create positive change.

Vivek Wadhwa

With deepest love and gratitude to my parents and my family and respect for my many teachers at CSC, Accenture, Capco, IBM, and now Capita. In memory of Hazrat, who shaped the lives of so many.

Ismail Amla

CONTENTS

Foreword ix
Preface xiii
Introduction: The Golden Age of Innovation Is Now 1

PART I
Why Exponential Disruptions Are Happening More Quickly and More Often

1 The Technological Basis of Breakthrough Disruption 13
2 The Unexpected Consequences of Advancing Technologies 21
3 The Old Innovator's Dilemma versus the New Innovator's Dilemma 32

PART II
Why Top-Down Innovation Efforts Usually Fail

4 False Assumptions, Broken Models, Wasted Effort 55
5 The Rules of the Game Have Changed in Critical Ways 72
6 What Has Not Changed 86
7 The Eight Deadly Sins That Disable Change Efforts 93

PART III
Ways to Build Innovative, Exponentially Developing Companies

8 "Don't Buy This Jacket": Subverting Retail Expectations 107

9 Platform Technologies and Marketplaces 111

10 How to (Dis)organize for Innovation 119

11 The Tactics of Innovative Companies 124

12 Change Management and Company Culture: An Innovation Manifesto 132

13 How to Recognize and Use the Strengths of Incumbency 144

14 From Dinosaurs to Eagles: Four Case Studies 153

15 Innovation Management in Government 174

Conclusion: You Can't Ignore It; How Can You Embrace It? 183

Notes 189

Index 201

Acknowledgements 213

About the Authors 215

Foreword

IT GIVES me immense pleasure to introduce Vivek Wadhwa's latest book, *From Incremental to Exponential.* He and his co-authors, with decades of experience behind them, have unboxed, explained and analyzed the leading theme of our times—innovation.

Vivek is a renowned thought leader in the technology space as well a distinguished academician. Based out of Silicon Valley, he is a Distinguished Fellow at Harvard Law School's Labor and Worklife Program. His elaborate body of work has unpacked the frontier technologies of robotics, artificial intelligence, computing, synthetic biology, 3D printing, medicine, and nanomaterials—and what it means for the most pressing issues of our time such as education, water, food, shelter, health, and security.

An award-winning writer and thinker, Vivek has worked for leading institutions such as Carnegie Mellon University, Duke University and Stanford Law School, among others. I value his opinion and insights on all things tech and so do many others. Vivek has been featured in Foreign Policy magazine's "Top 100 Global Thinkers" and TIME magazine's "Tech 40", and he was one of "ten men worth emulating" in the *Financial Times.* He is no stranger to writing best-sellers on topics close to his heart.

From Incremental to Exponential couldn't have come at a more opportune time—the world thought that it has harnessed the power of innovation but along came Covid-19, disrupting things we took for granted. Everyone was compelled to go back to the drawing board and work on innovative ways to navigate the post-Covid world. It has demonstrated that the future belongs to tech and digital innovations.

I personally found the key insights of the book extremely pertinent for today's age. The role of data that is widely and cheaply available and the emerging role of AI bode well for all of us. India's digital growth, in terms of the rising penetration of smartphone and cheapest mobile data in the world, offers the country immense scope for a technological revolution. There are lessons for governments and private companies, as he notes that technological disruption unleashes its own unintended consequences that are difficult to anticipate. We must appreciate that innovation can come from any direction, and so far as one is capable of absorbing and leveraging it, they stand to gain from it. In India, startups are using the power of Artificial Intelligence (AI) and Machine Learning (ML) to disrupt existing business models in education, health, and agriculture. Through sheer innovation they are transforming lives and enhancing productivity.

One of the most important takeaways for me is the strategies that have failed in fostering innovation in the past. It is only when one understands these cases that one may find solace that innovation doesn't lie at the end of a straight line or has a set formula. As India becomes one of the world's leading startup ecosystems with a domestic customer base of 1.3 billion, the section on how rules of innovation have changed becomes imperative for Indian entrepreneurs and politicians. If you want to create an impact at that scale, you need to be agile and highly cognizant of the shifting sands of the innovation game. This is well complemented by his insights on what slows down, or rather, negates innovation. For the world's third-biggest startup ecosystem, there are lessons galore.

As India aims to become the tech garage of the world and leverages technology to give benefits to the common man at his doorstep over the last decade, policymakers here should listen to Vivek's thoughts on platform technologies and marketplace. Though he speaks about the business world, the policymakers stand to benefit as much. He does a fine job of sharing the secret ingredients of innovative companies.

The section on the role of government in fostering innovation is something that is dear to me. We have been trying to create an enabling environment to boost innovation in India over the last few years. His lessons on government's role are simple but valuable.

The book's nuanced view on innovation is its biggest selling point. He doesn't claim anything that is not backed by evidence or case studies. In fact, the case studies make this book an accessible and enjoyable read, something that books on technology often fail to achieve.

I highly recommend this book to everyone—as technology touches our lives like never before. If we understand the innovation that goes behind what we see, we will appreciate the world around us much more. In particular, I recommend this book to Indian entrepreneurs and policymakers. We will benefit from listening to Vivek's insights on innovation. Post-Covid the need to innovate has received greater momentum. In understanding what works and what doesn't, relevant cases and the government's role, Vivek has done path-breaking work. It is now time for us to read, learn and imbibe these lessons.

Amitabh Kant
CEO, NITI Aayog
New Delhi
October 2020

Preface

WE, VIVEK and Ismail, have lived parallel existences in the technology world. One of us, Vivek, came up through the world of software and startups and has spent the last decade and a half as an academic. In that role, Vivek has advocated entrepreneurship and researched and taught on exponentially advancing technologies such as artificial intelligence (A.I.), computing, digital medicine, robots, sensors, synthetic biology, and quantum computing. Vivek often warned that incumbent megacorporations are soon to be "toast"; he was skeptical that they could adapt quickly enough to keep abreast of technology changes and compete with startups. Hoping he could help legacy companies that wanted to improve their chances of survival, Vivek created a methodology to teach big companies how to be more innovative using the very same tools and mindsets that foster hypergrowth in startups.

During the same period, Ismail focused on the world of technology consulting, working at large blue-chip firms such as IBM and Accenture. In those roles, he coached those same megacorporations in how to make better use of technology to improve their bottom lines and business processes. Ismail was teaching them how to avoid becoming toast.

And both of us learned how difficult it is to get megacorps to behave like startups.

But an interesting thing has happened over the past decade. We both began seeing clear signs of large, positive changes in the giant companies we advised. For his part, Vivek began spending more time with the giant corporations that he believed were facing extinction. He observed that some were not only surviving but even thriving. They were transforming themselves into innovation powerhouses, unconstrained by the traditional laws of large numbers. Initially, large tech companies such as Google and Microsoft had figured out how to scale up their innovation practices and maintain the type of agility and experimental environment that encourages continuous reinvention. Then a handful of legacy companies in the slowest-changing industries, such as Walmart and NextEra Energy, began to make real progress toward reinvention by embracing an innovation culture. Vivek was intrigued.

From the business side, Ismail felt change in the air when many of the large companies he was advising began to wield their strengths to spur innovation. Legacy companies may be slow and bureaucratic; yet Ismail noted that they also possess mountains of the most valuable currency of the 21st century: data. They also have highly experienced, networked executives and well-honed sales and marketing channels useful for distributing revolutionary new products. The most innovative of these legacy companies use the best practices of Silicon Valley to develop products and innovate rapidly; this lets them compete on an even footing—even at an advantage—with upstarts seeking to invade their turf.

For example, in December 2018, online retailer Amazon made clear it had plans to bring its automated, cashierless Amazon Go stores to the United Kingdom in the near future.[1] Shortly thereafter, Sainsbury's, the largest incumbent British grocery conglomerate, announced that it would be launching a similar concept.[2] In fact, Sainsbury's executives had long been exploring cashierless technology and planning for precisely this event. Recognizing Amazon as an existential threat, the grocery giant activated its innovation plan and adopted a mindset that allowed it to move quickly and embrace newer technologies—something that grocery chains are hardly known for.

Such breakthrough responses represent trends and provide paradigms that we believe can benefit legacy enterprises, very few of which have mined the rich vein of thought, strategy, and opportunity that many startups and other innovative companies have pioneered. While this book is written primarily for executives and managers at these legacy companies, in reality anyone who wants to learn about applied innovation can benefit by applying the analytical approaches and innovation tools that the innovators have invented.

Some executives and managers have already familiarized themselves with the successes of Google, eBay, PayPal, and Facebook. Very few, though, are up-to-date on the newer-generation disruptors such as Tencent, Zoom, Airbnb, and Deliveroo and their best practices for innovation and agility. Understanding these approaches can empower large organizations from public institutions to nonprofits and social enterprises as well as corporations to rapidly adopt methods and mindsets that will enable them to increase their growth by making them more responsive to their environment.

Our real hope for this book is that it will help the leaders and employees of these organizations boost their innovation metabolism—and engender a transformation that eliminates the distinction between startup and incumbent.

We hope too to make evident that genuinely sustainable innovation entails attention to its ethics and to its potential to provide social benefit and uplift humanity. Growth generally creates prosperity for companies, employees, and shareholders, but the enterprise's genuine longevity depends on genuine responsibility. Technology and innovation without consideration can lead to highly unpleasant outcomes.[3] Modern technology and innovation make incredible things possible; it matters that we use them in a sensible and equitable way rather than merely as a means to profits and revenues. It is the authors' hope that, in learning to recapture the spring of their early growth, legacy companies at risk of being overshadowed by upstarts will find themselves on fresh ground, ready to undertake the kind of growth that will make the world a better place.

Introduction

The Golden Age of Innovation Is Now

ON APRIL 11, 2019, a Falcon Heavy rocket, as it rose in the early-morning light from its launchpad at Cape Canaveral, Florida, made history.[1] This windswept spaceport on the Atlantic Coast has served as the launchpad for innovation in space since the 1960s—the Apollo moon missions and the Space Shuttle missions all blasted off from here.

But the Falcon Heavy was designed not only to transport cargo into space but also to recover all three of its primary rocket boosters. Each booster would pilot itself back to touchdown, the twin side boosters on launchpads at Canaveral and the larger center booster upright on a bobbing barge in the middle of the ocean.[2] SpaceX also caught discarded rocket fairings (nose cones) before they hit the Atlantic. All of these components were to be re-used in future launches.

The company behind the FalconX was not one of the legacy giants of spaceflight—Boeing or Arianespace or Roscosmos. The FalconX was designed and manufactured by SpaceX, a relative newcomer founded by billionaire Elon Musk.

Upon hearing about SpaceX's intention to build reusable rockets, the aerospace world collectively concluded that Musk and his engineers were crazy to attempt such a difficult feat. For the team at SpaceX, though, the calculus was straightforward. Rocket launches cost too much, making the market for rocket launches and everything else in space smaller and less attractive. The cost of access to space made it the sole province of large multinationals and governments that could afford to pay hundreds of millions of dollars to put satellites into orbit. Reusing key rocket components would reduce that price tag by 20 percent to 40 percent, depending on how much of the savings SpaceX passed on to customers.[3]

By creating a cheaper way to launch rockets and put cargo into space, SpaceX could take on the incumbents and radically expand the market for launches, satellites, and everything else space related. Its technology and cost advantage would create opportunities for thousands of other companies. Such platforms give technology companies such as Apple, Facebook, and Google an enormous strategic and financial advantage. The challenge the SpaceX engineers aimed to surmount was ludicrously difficult: to guide three multi-ton rockets back to a gentle Earth landing with pinpoint accuracy.

But, on April 11, 2019, SpaceX did just that.

SpaceX's success leads to two obvious questions:

How was a young and relatively small company able to achieve such a feat?

Why hadn't the larger, well-capitalized aerospace companies attempted and succeeded with something similar?

To answer the first question, let's consider what factors made SpaceX possible. Before the Internet era, the skepticism that would have greeted an upstart company attempting to build a reusable rocket would have made a struggle of the attempt to raise the billions of dollars in funding necessary for building prototypes and performing research. Funding on that scale at that time was largely reserved for drug and medical-device development. In fact, such large capital funding for startups has generally been rare other than at the dawn of the aviation and automobile ages in the 1920s and 1930s, when a host of smaller companies raised significant capital. Once in a blue moon, a startup has attempted to crack a capital-intensive industry. DeLorean Motors, the maker of elegant gull-winged stainless steel sports cars, briefly succeeded; but it was a clear exception.

In its short eighteen-year existence, SpaceX has found many ways to raise capital from a vast and growing pool of investors eager to back risky but potentially lucrative ventures. The capital has sufficed because companies such as SpaceX can now stretch it farther than was possible earlier.

For example, SpaceX was easily able to acquire technological infrastructure sufficient to undercut incumbents in the conception, testing, and production of complicated rockets. It benefited from cloud computing, open-source software, and many other technology innovations that have slashed the cost of starting a company to which advanced technologies are so central. Because SpaceX was not restrained by legacy biases or by the established behaviors common to incumbents, the upstart was able to ingest and deploy many of the acceleration mechanisms that fast-growing technology companies have used to leapfrog older competitors.

At the same time, SpaceX had far less trouble in recruiting the talent necessary to undertake its quest than it might have decades ago, when taking a large risk on a startup was perceived as career suicide. Today, legacy companies prize startup experience—and that minimizes the employee's risk of becoming unemployable should the startup fizzle.

To sum up, SpaceX benefited from a confluence of capital-market changes, technology changes, and changes in employer culture. These changes allowed it to launch and fly fast.

The second question is why none of the larger, well-capitalized aerospace companies have attempted something similar.

Engineers at Boeing were no less intelligent and accomplished than the team at SpaceX, and Boeing lacked neither resources nor ambition.

In fact, the company remains a leader in numerous manufacturing and process technologies, such as using augmented reality to reduce complexity and errors in the assembly of increasingly complex airplanes.[4] And surely Boeing or one of the other aerospace giants has considered the concept of reusable rockets. More broadly, every company of any size would argue that it prizes and strives for innovation, particularly since the term came into vogue in the past 40 years. Yet a chasm separates companies such as SpaceX from Boeing, Airbus, and Lockheed Martin, and it is unclear whether companies such as Boeing even understand that they have to innovate more rapidly in order to survive. Something has prevented these companies from unleashing their mighty potential to transform their business quickly, to respond to new threats, and to adopt the tactics and ideas of fast-growing younger companies.

The obstacles are hiding in plain sight, and they all share the same mindset: a mindset of "No" as opposed to "Grow!" All too often, employees in the legacy companies struggle to embrace the new—and so helplessly look on as upstarts blaze new paths that capture their markets by offering greater value.

The technology for men's razor blades (despite hyperbolic advertising claims) has remained unchanged for 50 years: thin blades are placed in plastic or steel cartridges, sent in shrink-wrapped packages or plastic boxes to a store. They have been licenses to print money. Many a business school use the "razors and razor blades" case studies to illustrate seeding lucrative markets by giving away the tool and banking on the purchase of refills.

Yet, with one cheeky video and an in-your-face marketing campaign, Dollar Shave Club made razor blades exciting again—or at least somewhat convenient—once the company caught your attention (with its hilarious CEO striding briskly through his warehouse, tie askew, drolly extolling the virtues of his blades).

Dollar Shave Club didn't innovate in razor blades. In fact, according to third-party review sites such as Wirecutter (owned by *The New*

York Times), its blades are no higher in quality than Gillette's or other blade makers'.[5] Rather, its innovation lay in its bold and brassy go-to-market strategy that a confluence of modern developments made possible: YouTube, as one of the world's largest video publishers and advertising platforms; the preference of millennials (and increasingly others) to subscribe to delivery services rather than buy in the store; and the emergence of Google AdWords and other online advertising platforms that democratized marketing channels and proved a fast and economical way to drive business.

A decade earlier, getting a new razor blade into major distribution channels would have entailed paying massive slotting fees to supermarkets and pharmacies and going toe-to-toe with giant consumer packaged-goods brands on their home turf, with no clear advantage. But a smart YouTube video that cost Dollar Shave Club $4,500 to make received millions of views,[6] vaulting Dollar Shave Club into the broad consumer consciousness overnight.[7] And, in less than five years, from 2012 to 2017, Dollar Shave Club's U.S. market share in shaving products rose to 7 percent of sales overall and 30 percent in e-commerce, with nearly $200 million in annual sales, reducing the market share of the market leader, Procter & Gamble's Gillette, from 70 percent to less than 50 percent.[8] This terrified the incumbents, who had put little energy into converting their casual sales into regular subscriptions. Yet Gillette could have mounted a tongue-in-check effort to capture e-commerce and disrupt its own cozy market for men's shaving products.

Dollar Shave Club's campaign was an example of exponentially effective innovation in marketing through new consumer sales and communication channels. Though less technologically impressive than SpaceX's achievements, Dollar Shave Club's was an amazing feat in its own right: creating a billion-dollar company in five short years in a legacy space with an unremarkable product. In 2017, consumer goods giant Unilever purchased the company for $1 billion.[9]

Gillette woke up just in time and launched a subscription business that recognized Amazon's growing preference for subscriptions to consumer products. (Amazon conveniently adds a "Subscribe to" option for most consumer product purchases.) Gillette now competes on a nearly even footing with Dollar Shave Club and will not lose everything in the market for men's shaving products. It may even regain its dominance and crush Dollar Shave Club—but we would not bet on that, for reasons you'll read about later on in this book. We would imagine instead that Gillette will apply the lesson to the creation of more brands and smarter go-to-market strategies—competing on an even footing with the upstarts by appropriating their methods. (At least, we hope it will if its executives read this book.)

During our exploration, we will look to SpaceX, Dollar Shave Club, and other upstarts whose breakthrough innovation and growth have taken advantage of the new realities in technology, society, and business. We will see how a legacy U.S. energy-generation company, NextEra Energy, managed to significantly improve its growth prospects and to future-proof itself by taking note of exponential developments and resolutely turning its focus to renewables, all without disrupting its legacy business. We will study how a legacy technology company, Microsoft, rebooted innovation by transforming its culture. And we will look at the compounding effects of multiple changes in the way the world works and at how these changes fundamentally alter how companies interact with customers and consumers.

It is in these very changes that the roots of rapid transformation and the keys to breakthrough innovation lie. From the printing press to the internal-combustion engine to transistors and electricity to computer chips and all the ensuing advancements, the pace of change is accelerating—not only because the technology is becoming more effective, but also because startups are more effectively executing their visions, and because a growing number of larger corporations are now adopting their tactics and strategies and achieving similar or even better results.

Realistically, although we are seeking to use timeless examples in this book, many of our illustrations may seem dated within 18 months of printing; that is, in part, the nature of the beast, and of our perceptions too. What remains timeless, however, is a logical approach to applying the best tools of change and innovation inside older organizations: those whose established processes and products may be their very vulnerabilities.

Along these lines, we also want to show that all too many legacy companies' views of innovation have been colored by a dilemma in which competing with the newcomers and growing will require disrupting themselves. The dilemma is illusory. Legacy companies have tremendous advantages in scale, knowledge, data, sales channels, marketing machines, brand, and relationships. They can disrupt by using those advantages.

In this book, we aim not only to cover many examples and delve into what works and what does not, but also to provide you with an innovation tool kit that you can apply to your organization. We will cover some of the new techniques that "platform" companies such as Google, Facebook, and Apple use. We will look at how large organizations can think and act like startups. We will take you on a whirlwind tour of some of the most engaging means by which the smartest companies are succeeding at innovating, from internal science fairs to design sprints to innovation prizes.

None of this book's messages apply only to the for-profit sector. The book is designed to help any organization that wants to hone its innovation chops. We hope you and your organization find the book useful in effecting greater innovation—and greater success.

PART I

Why Exponential Disruptions Are Happening More Quickly and More Often

When reports emerged in January 2020 from China of a novel disease that spread like the flu but seemed far more lethal, the world's scientific community kicked into high gear. Researchers in China used high-speed genetic-sequencing equipment to sequence the genome of the novel coronavirus associated with the disease and posted the genome online so that scientists everywhere could study it. As evidence of infection by the virus and familiarity with the disease's symptoms quickly spread, scientists compressed into a few months procedures that usually take years, including efforts to identify existing medicines that ameliorate COVID-19's worst effects, randomized clinical trials, and preliminary vaccine research. This was a manifestation of the power of computing and the massive transformation that silicon has wrought in the life sciences. What used to cost billions of dollars and require teams of scientists—such as sequencing a human genome—now can be done in an hour with an automated sequencing machine for less than $500.

We also got a glimpse of what the future might hold for us as a massively connected society. Hundreds of millions who had been studying face-to-face in schools, technical colleges, and tertiary institutions began distance learning, studying from home with peers and teachers via videoconferencing, an early version of what might finally take shape as virtual reality (V.R.) classrooms in which every class member is present though not physically in the same room. Huge swathes of society learned how to use videoconferencing tools to build connections and became comfortable having meetings, going to church, and celebrating birthdays over the Internet.

The power of collective existence came into clear focus. Kinsa, a company tracking the temperature of more than a million U.S. users of digital thermometers linked to smartphones, collected data on unusual clusters of fever that were detectable in the early stages, hinting at how our devices collectively may become a de facto pandemic early-warning system, superior even to existing detection methods.[1] Dr. Eric Topol, a renowned physician and advocate for digital health and A.I. applications in health care, launched a large-scale trial to test whether Apple Watches could be used to identify virus hot spots by measuring increases in their wearers' resting heart rates. On the more radical front, researchers unveiled plans for a system to spot early signs of COVID-19 outbreaks by monitoring sewage systems for genetic evidence of the virus.

Digital thermometers, online grocery shopping, and delivery drones (to alleviate the painful shipping bottlenecks that slowed package delivery) exemplify the new ways of living, shopping, working, and playing that we adopted almost overnight. Whether these shifts are permanent remains to be seen. But the speed with which society took up new technologies, adapted cultural and economic activity, and accelerated efforts to work toward a cure and a relevant vaccine was mind-boggling. And it was possible only because the underlying conditions for rapid technology-driven changes existed and were accessible to billions of people on Earth. This section reviews the technological and cultural stimuli of the most innovative of these changes and outlines the challenges that established enterprises most commonly face in attempting to remain viable in the face of them.

1

The Technological Basis of Breakthrough Disruption

CHAPTER SUMMARY: This chapter covers what happens as information becomes widely and cheaply available. Using how Uber benefited from Google Maps and soaring smartphone usage, we discuss how the next wave of disruption is coming from artificial intelligence (A.I.) making good predictions cheap or free. The chapter details how the rapidly falling costs of technologies such as computer chips, sensors, and network capacity, are increasingly enabling broader possibilities, such as the ubiquity of the smartphone.

TO OBTAIN a license to pilot a black cab in London, applicants must pass an incredibly difficult exam called *the Knowledge*. The exam requires them to show that they have memorized the Byzantine street layout of the British capital and can calculate the most efficient path from point A to point B at any given time of day. Navigating London's chaotic and unpredictable arterial streets and congested roundabouts is challenging, and drivers able to demonstrate such ability were paid relatively well, considering that this was not an advanced professional degree. This made the job of driving a black cab highly desirable.

Then Uber entered the market. The prominence of black cabs entered a steep decline as Uber grabbed market share through its cheaper fares and its ubiquity. But a quick look under the hood reveals something more: Uber didn't disrupt black cabs all by itself. Google Maps played an equally central role in its demise. Google Maps effectively made the Knowledge available—for free—to anyone with a smartphone, and Uber initially used Google Maps for turn-by-turn navigation for its drivers. It is likely that, had it arrived without a means of minimizing the importance of the Knowledge, Uber would not have succeeded.[1]

By making available for free (or nearly free) cartographic information that had been expensive and hard to obtain, Google affected a wide variety of companies that depended on the value of geographical information, from navigation device makers such as Garmin and TomTom to the sellers of geographic data such as Telenav. As an indication of the disruption that Google Maps and the emergence of free turn-by-turn apps on smartphones caused: Garmin's market capitalization, which in September 2007 was more than $16 billion, went into freefall when Google Maps became available, plummeting to the $2 billion range. It took Garmin a long 12 years to regain a $16 billion market capitalization,[2] which it did by transforming its entire business model and locating alternative revenue sources beyond its formerly dominant turn-by-turn navigation systems.[3]

This pattern is common to breakthrough disruptions. Unlike the days in which the disruption came from a cheaper product's crashing the market at the lower end, the new form of industry disruptions makes key business activities nearly free or incredibly cost effective, enabling upstarts to very quickly enter and capture market share or to build entirely new businesses on the new economics these disruptions enable.

In many fields, accurate predictions were formerly very expensive, if not impossible. Predictions are becoming far more affordable and often free—through the analysis of mountains of data that we already have, through the use of technologies such as A.I. As economists Ajay Agrawal, Joshua Gans, and Avi Goldfarb explain in their book *Prediction Machines: The Simple Economics of Artificial Intelligence,* freely available predictions will fundamentally change how we conduct our lives and how business behaves:

> Having better prediction raises the value of judgment. After all, it doesn't help to know the likelihood of rain if you don't know how much you like staying dry or how much you hate carrying an umbrella. Prediction machines don't provide judgment. Only humans do, because only humans can express the relative rewards from taking different actions. As A.I. takes over prediction, humans will do less of the combined prediction-judgment routine of decision making and focus more on the judgment role alone.[4]

Although A.I. is (contrary to popular belief) nowhere near replacing human intelligence, free predictions will enable the humans who embrace its capabilities to make faster and more effective decisions.

The case of Uber, black cabs, and the Knowledge made a clear analogy a decade before A.I. began making predictions free. Geographic knowledge at any significant scale before the rise of computing, satellites, cheaper sensors, ubiquitous connectivity, and high-speed wireless networks was dear. Further back in time, in the days of Christopher Columbus and Amerigo Vespucci, the maps that held geographic knowledge determined the wealth of nations. Today, knowledge is becoming far less expensive, and more knowledge is accumulating at a dizzying pace. This accumulation would be crippling if not for the rise of A.I. With A.I., we can make sense of much of this noise.

Thus, A.I. and its impact on predictions—and subsequently on business—are the tip of the spear of exponential disruption.

Sensors, Chips, Software: How Exponential Technologies Combine to Become Breakthrough Innovations

The common perception that the technology world is moving ever faster is not wrong: adoption of newer generations of technology is occurring more quickly today than fifty or even twenty years ago. Earlier technologies with the potential to transform our world, such as the steam engine and electricity, required as long as a century to attain widespread use. Radios and televisions penetrated more quickly than electricity did, but widespread adoption of each took several decades. From the emergence of the computer to nearly 90 percent penetration took about two decades. The smartphone's far more global penetration took a single decade. The adoption of newer technologies, such as voice assistants, is even faster, with significant uptake occurring in roughly five years. A.I. too, although it had been bubbling in the background for decades, went from nascent to nearly omnipresent in roughly five years.

So yes, everything is moving faster, and the pace of change is accelerating. A.I. will help us understand what is going on around us and to make predictions, making a scarce good or service free. The cost of clean energy will fall to a point at which it seems free. Everyone on Earth who wants an Internet-connected smartphone or V.R. headset will have one, giving us a truly global span for information sharing. The platforms supporting such technology are also getting faster. Emerging 5G wireless networks, modern WiFi, and giant fleets of cheap communication satellites launched into low-Earth orbit will provide fast broadband everywhere for a fraction of the current costs of electronic communication. The scramble for A.I. is driving a new wave of computer-chip startups seeking to address problems of machine learning, and the resulting chip designs hold tremendous promise for performing computing tasks far more efficiently and elegantly than occurs now. Impediments to innovation and rapid technological acceleration are falling away as speeds rise, costs fall, and adoption quickens.

The human genome is a case in point. Sequencing the first human genome cost roughly $2.7 billion: a tremendous effort involving large teams of scientists and labs full of equipment. This occurred in the year 2000, as a result of a thirteen-year government-led effort.[5] Today, some labs can fully sequence a human genome for less than $1,000; the cost will fall below $25 in less than a decade, as a result of improved technologies for DNA analysis: a highly automated process running on laboratory tools that are essentially high-speed computers using cheap sensors to prise open and analyze the formerly mysterious double helix that is the recipe book of life.

What Is Driving Exponential Innovation

In their book *The Driver in the Driverless Car,* Vivek Wadhwa and Alex Salkever detail a range of technologies that are advancing on an exponential curve and the possibilities they have enabled. These diverse technologies are also converging. This convergence, or combination, creates opportunities for entrepreneurs to disrupt entire industries.

You have seen the advances in our computers, how they keep getting faster and smaller. The Cray supercomputers of the 1970s were considered strategic government assets. They could not be exported; they were for scientific research and defense; and they cost tens of millions of dollars. They needed to be housed in huge buildings and required water cooling. The smartphones many of us carry in our pockets are many times more powerful than the Crays were.

This progression follows an industrywide development cycle known as *Moore's law.* For more than half a century, the speed, efficiency, cost-effectiveness, and power of computing devices has doubled roughly every 18 months. Faster computers are now used to design even faster computers; and computers—and the information technology (I.T.)

they enable—are absorbing other fields. The result is exponential advances in sensors, A.I., robotics, medicine, 3D printing, and more. To paraphrase futurist and inventor Ray Kurzweil, as any technology becomes an information technology, it starts advancing exponentially.

The advances in sensors such as the camera on a smartphone are illustrative. Kodak introduced the first "computerized" camera in 1976. It weighed 4 pounds, cost $10,000, and had a resolution of a whopping 0.01 megapixels. Today, the cameras in some mobile phones have 108-megapixel photosensors, and the cameras are merely an extra. You may remember, too, the really expensive high-definition cameras that film studios started using at the turn of the century. Apple's iPhones from the iPhone 9 Plus to the iPhone 11 shoot video at four times the resolution (3,840 x 2,160 pixels) of those early professional cameras. Similar advances have occurred in other types of sensors: in accelerometers; gyroscopes; and sensors of temperature, gas, humidity; as well as in microfluidics[6] and in the performance of chemical and biological tests on small, inexpensive chips.

Sensors' improvements in accuracy and reductions in price are also facilitating a revolution in manufacturing, in which their rapid spread (the "Industrial Internet of Things") has enabled what many now term *Industry 4.0,* rapidly raising manufacturing processes' efficiency by capturing data on every key variable of production: pressure, temperature, ambient humidity, percentage of scrap, precision of casts—you name it. This information gives factory processes digital souls that are transparent and tunable, almost like software code. Like the smartphone, Industry 4.0 became possible when multiple elements—sensors, connectivity, computing power—became cheap, powerful, and compact.

It's when exponentially advancing technologies combine that the magic happens. Such convergence makes possible new applications and allows the creation of new industries at the cost of the older ones.

If we take the data we are collecting from sensors, the Internet, and the computerization of almost all knowledge work and apply A.I. to their analysis, we obtain the ability to predict traffic patterns, crime, sales, and trends.

Computers will also soon be performing medical diagnoses. The Apple Watch and Fitbit are medical devices that use advanced sensors to monitor our health. Thousands of such medical sensors are in development worldwide. They will monitor our activity levels and our sleep; our vital signs and body fluids: everything about us. A.I. systems in the form of smartphone apps will read these data 24/7. They will advise us when we are about to fall ill and will recommend better lifestyles, habits, and treatments. These technologies are becoming possible because of the combination of sensors, computing, medical libraries, and A.I. We now even have sensors, such as SugarBEAT from Nemaura, entering the market that will allow non-invasive glucose monitoring, changing the lives of hundreds of millions of diabetics in the world. In a decade or so, we will not need doctors to advise us on day-to-day health; their work will be for the complicated ailments. These incredible technologies will disrupt the entire medical industry.

The Limits of Technology

When we were young, many of us watched TV shows such as *Star Trek* and dreamed of replicators—which would produce all the icecream and dessert we could eat—or of having a robotic assistant like Rosie from *The Jetsons* clean up after us. But Rosie never came, and all we've had by way of replicators are 3D printers that print cheap plastic toys. Indeed, the most advanced robots in our homes today are Roombas—pathetic little automated vacuum cleaners. (Yes, we know that some people love their Roombas!)

Why No Rosie?

There is no Rosie because the computation power required for a robot to recognize voices and speak intelligently would have required a Cray computer, and the sensors—camera, motion detectors, gyroscopes, accelerometers—were too bulky and expensive.

Guess what a smartphone can do today, though: all of that, and much more.

Rosie has become possible, and it is conceivable that Amazon will deliver her to our homes by drone in the late 2020s. We'll also see robots doing the jobs of humans in manufacturing plants, grocery stores, and pharmacies. And they will be driving cars and making deliveries. Robots will soon do all the routine things that humans do. Imagine the resulting possibilities and disruptions.

Replicators too are on their way. There are already demonstrations of "3D-printed" meat and desserts by startups in many countries. We will be 3D printing not only food but also cars, electronics, houses, and space stations.

Every industry in which technology can be applied or that generates data faces these advances. There may be no industry whose leading players won't face economic extinction.

It is important to acknowledge that, although advancing technologies enable a lot of good, they also enable large-scale destruction, spying, and unimaginable horrors. Already creating social and ethical dilemmas, they are taking us into a future in which there won't be much work in the professions of today and we'll have to figure out what to do with ourselves. There will surely be social unrest as the rate of change accelerates and the gap between the haves and have-nots widens; there will also be efforts to halt the progress of certain technologies. If we are to be masters rather than victims of our tools, this ever-present choice of futures (the key message of *The Driver in the Driverless Car*) is one we must come to grips with.

2

The Unexpected Consequences of Advancing Technologies

CHAPTER SUMMARY: After touching on our understanding of the broad influences on technology adoption, this chapter discusses how primary (first-order) disruptions usually lead to second-order disruptions, including new business models and new means by which businesses, governments, and nonprofits can interact with customers. The chapter also offers a glimpse into the "Hall of Toast" through a series of case studies and analyses documenting how once high-flying companies have gone astray when faced with disruptive technological shifts.

IN 1995, the American research, advisory, and I.T. firm Gartner created a concept it called the Hype Cycle (Figure 2.1).[1] Broadly adopted and embraced since by the business and analyst community, the Gartner Hype Cycle is a model showing rough timelines and stages in the maturation, adoption, and social application of technologies. Though it has been deprecated as inaccurate and lacking a basis in evidence, the Hype Cycle does provide a useful framework for thinking about technology adoption.

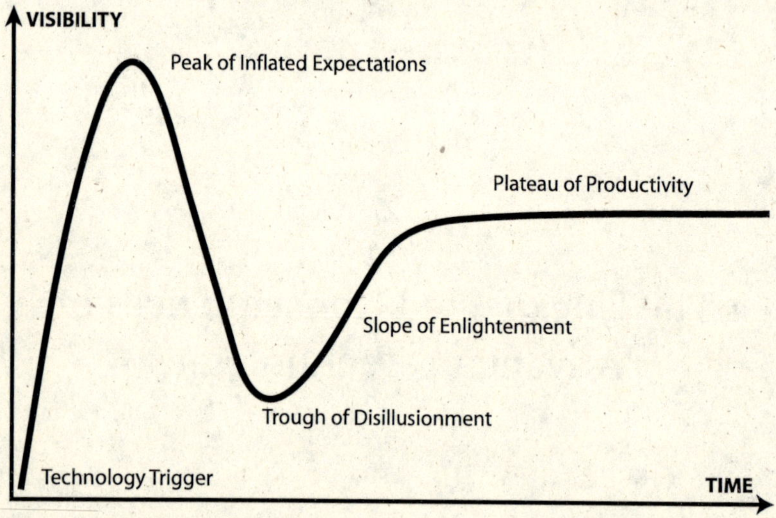

Figure 2.1. The Hype Cycle model for technology adoption created by technology research and analyst company Gartner, Inc.

Source: Gartner, Inc. (https://commons.wikimedia.org/wiki/Category:Hype_cycle#/media/ File:Gartner_Hype_Cycle.svg)

In the field of V.R., for example, there was enormous hype (the "Peak of Inflated Expectations" in the Hype Cycle) leading to breathless predictions about people living most of their lives in virtual environments, followed by caustic articles (the "Trough of Disillusionment") about early-generation V.R. goggles making people seasick. Now we appear to be moving up the curve's "Slope of Enlightenment" as applications of V.R. gear are emerging and people who are not early adopters are using them to do nifty things such as sit "courtside" at professional basketball games in the United States. In the very near future, we will hit the curve's "Plateau of Productivity"—the point at which V.R. has become part of everyday life and is no longer rare or unusual. Among smartphones, the iPhone brought us to this point; among computers, the Mac and Windows computers did. A useful test of whether a technology has hit this point is whether something "just works" with almost no effort or learning curve—in the way in which an experienced user of earlier mobile phones can pick up an iPhone and immediately understand how to operate it.

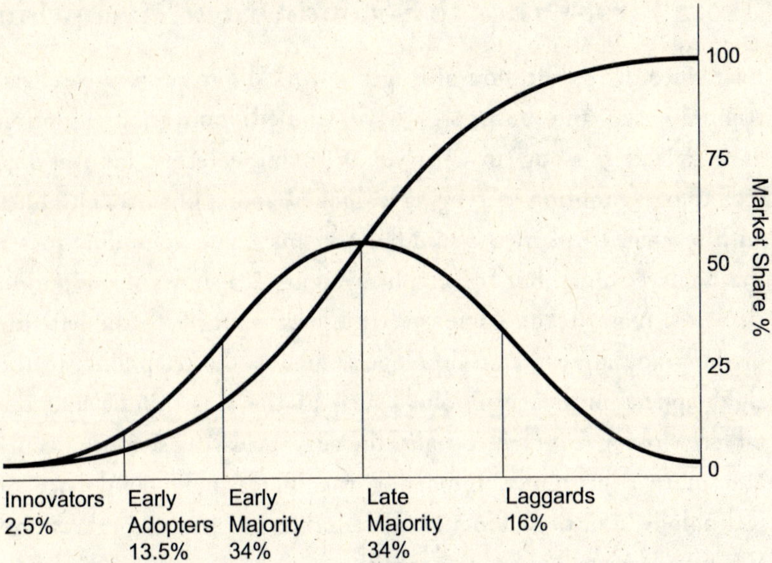

Figure 2.2. Rogers's Diffusion of Innovation Model. In his 1962 book *Diffusion of Innovations,* Everett Rogers popularized the theory that explains how, why, and at what rate new ideas and technology spread.

Adapted from Everett Rogers, *Diffusion of Innovations,* London and New York: Free Press, 1962 (https://en.wikipedia.org/wiki/File:Diffusion_of_ideas.svg)

A more robust (albeit drier) model of technology adoption is Everett Rogers's Innovation Diffusion Model (Figure 2.2).[2] The model attempts to explain why, how, and at what pace new technology and innovation spread. Rogers, a communications professor, first published this idea in a book in 1962. He takes a social contagion approach to innovation diffusion and technology spread, asserting that diffusion consists of four primary elements: the innovation itself; communication channels; time; and a social system. He posits that, in order to become self-sustaining, innovation must be widely adopted. He divides the adopters into five categories: innovators, early adopters, early majority, late majority, and laggards—the same categories that Geoffrey Moore uses in his iconic business book, *Crossing the Chasm.*

From First-Order to Second-Order Disruption

Ever since the publication of Rogers's work, innovation researchers, technologists, and businesses have studied innovation adoption as a trajectory along an S-curve. With more recent innovations, technology-adoption curves have looked more like straight lines with a small bend in the middle. You may have to squint to see the S-curves on it, but the graph in Figure 2.3 shows the adoption curves of major technologies over the past century. To the left side of the graph are earlier technologies, such as the telephone; to the right appear more recent ones, such as the smartphone and the tablet. Moving from left to right, the curves clearly rise more steeply and more consistently, indicating the increasingly rapid pace of technology adoption. Plots of the adoption of smart speakers and V.R. would have looked steeper still.

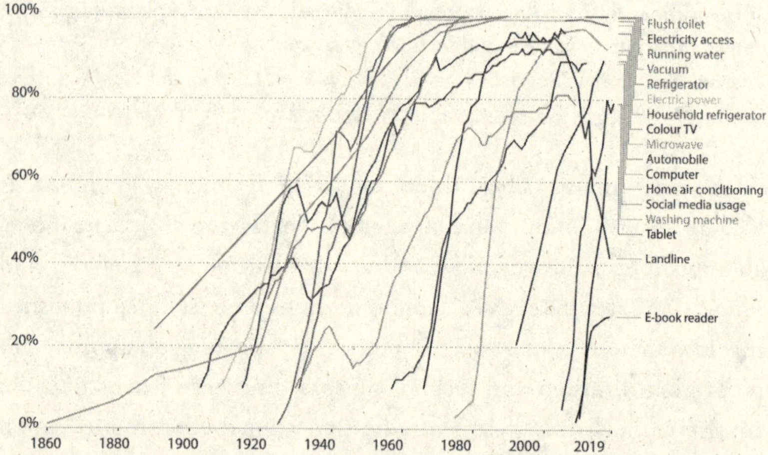

Figure 2.3. Accelerating Pace of Technology. Adoption rate of new technologies over time with adoption curves steepening (adoption growing more rapidly) from left to right.

Source: Our World in Data, https://ourworldindata.org/technology-adoption.

The acceleration in adoption of newer technologies is evidence of what we may call *second-order* disruption arising from breakthrough innovations. When multiple fast-moving (or exponentially advancing) technologies merge into one product class, the result is even faster development and improvement. Naturally, faster development and improvement mean faster maturation, which in turn generates swifter adoption.

Let's consider a few technologies in this light. The telephone, which proved to be a revolutionary device, used a single innovative technology—the conversion of electrical signals into sound and vice versa. The smartphone was a far more powerful technology. It incorporated a number of key legacy technologies—camera, telephone, typewriter, maps—and included overlapping exponentially advancing technologies, such as semiconductors, software, geolocation, and cheap sensors. Whereas the telephone is useful for communication, the smartphone, incorporating many exponentially advancing technologies, quickly became a tool without which many of us would be incapable of managing our lives—as well as one that consumes an ever-growing portion of our time.

The smartphone is today the dominant technology platform and continues to replace discrete devices and services at a voracious pace. Smartphones now carry the software and sensor equivalents of dozens of discrete consumer electronic devices, each representing a formerly lucrative and substantial market: the camera, the tape recorder, the telephone, the turn-by-turn GPS unit, the blood-oxygen sensor and heart-rate monitor, the fitness tracker, the stopwatch, the electronic (and physical) tape measure, and the DVD player. The list continues to grow as our phones gain utility via faster, more powerful computers and a wider array of cheap yet accurate sensors.

Until recently, however, the smartphone did not have a way to recognize complex patterns in the myriad data now appearing in our digital lives. This explains in part why Alexa and Amazon's voice services have taken off so quickly: they combine not only a useful range of exponential technologies but also well-designed predictive and pattern-matching software in the form of A.I. As machine learning becomes increasingly embedded into the technology we use, it will evolve faster and improve more quickly. A case in point is Tesla: the fact that it is both a car company and an A.I. company improving its systems and software using data gathered as its vehicles use the road is what underlies the company's ability to make the Tesla experience so magical.

The accelerating pace of innovation leads, unsurprisingly, to more opportunities for industry disruptions. A case in point is package delivery.

A Case Study in Exponential Disruption: Package Delivery

Delivery fleets have traditionally required planes, large trucks, boats, trains, and final-hop vehicles such as delivery vans, cars, and bicycle couriers. Buying or leasing the infrastructure for such a network was very expensive and capital intensive; and creating software to manage these networks required constantly updated map data, traffic information, and logistics and planning capabilities. Clearly those barriers have begun to fall: Uber, Lyft, Postmates, Deliveroo, and Grubhub have all either taken advantage of extant geolocation and mapping capabilities, logistics and dispatching software, and pricing algorithms or built their own—and have reached a nearly global scale in their first five years.

With the Federal Aviation Authority's approval of drones for delivery, the entire package-delivery model is about to receive an upgrade. Drones have tremendous advantages over cars and trucks: they have zero emissions; they never get stuck in traffic; they have a smaller form factor; and they don't require an accompanying human. Also, their cost is plummeting, and consumer-grade technology almost meets the requirements of commercial drones. (Drones are like smartphones with rotors. They use the same chips, sensors, and connectivity mechanisms.) And, whereas a Sprinter-style delivery van costs $50,000 or more, the cost of the latest iteration of self-flying autonomous drones has fallen below $1,000.

The use of drones fundamentally alters the pattern of goods transportation, ripening the market for innovation and exploration both by startups and by the faster-moving of the legacy companies. Drone development represents second-order innovation, having benefited from a confluence of smaller and cheaper computers, smaller and much cheaper sensors, essentially free geolocation data, and ubiquitous broadband connectivity. Drones may also alter the way factories work, by providing flying visual quality control and process analysis without the need to install and wire cameras at every corner of a production line: a flying version of Industry 4.0.

Faster technology development is a blessing and a curse for legacy companies: they have the resources to invest sooner than others in a technology, but their greater inertia tends to delay early adoption. An organization's ability to forgo overly rigid structures and hierarchies and to embrace change in how people work and think, remaking itself as needed, makes it more agile and less fragile than otherwise. The leaders of such organizations trust their smart employees to lead the way. And their CEOs ensure that their companies spend organizational, financial, and intellectual capital wisely: either on creating new business lines or on reinventing the future of existing business by rapidly adopting better technologies—even if those technologies may be unprofitable at first. In some scenarios, allowing spin-offs to chase innovation is a wise strategy. RCA, for instance, was spun off from General Electric in order to comply with U.S. antitrust laws.

For those organizations unable to adapt or change to embrace innovation, the Hall of Toast awaits.

The Hall of Toast and Modern Disruptors

Technology is obviously disrupting the status quo in business. Unsurprisingly, this is showing up in company balance sheets. Since 1935, the average duration of membership in the Standard & Poor's

500 has fallen from 90 years to less than 20 years, and it continues to fall. At the current rate of turnover, a full 75 percent of the current S&P 500 will be replaced in less than a decade. The majority of those that are pushed out of the S&P 500 will ultimately be consigned to oblivion or be snapped up by rivals or up-and-coming brands.

Companies that have fallen include iconic brands such RadioShack, Sears, Compaq, Yahoo, and Dell EMC. Others that may be on the way out include Hewlett-Packard, Gap, and Kraft Heinz. Still other giant brands have been subsumed, including Jaguar, Land Rover, Chrysler, Whole Foods, and America Online. Few remember any longer that RCA (Radio Corporation of America) was a dominant player in the market for early consumer electronics in radios and televisions through the 1970s and, in its day, boasted the most innovative productive invention labs in the world.

The Hall of Toast is replete with once-amazing legacy companies that failed to adapt quickly enough to exponential technologies on the horizon—even when they themselves had introduced the disruptive technologies. The classic Hall of Toast example is the camera and film company Kodak, which, founded in 1888, employed, at its peak, more than 120,000 people and was one of the most valuable companies in the world.

To its credit, Kodak had aggressively pursued smart research and development. In 1987, Kodak entered the "filmless" (or digital) camera market and later created a number of products for digital photography.

Wall Street thought that the company could do no wrong, tripling Kodak's share price even as the company announced cost-cutting plans with increasing frequency. The cash-cow film business afforded Kodak tremendous latitude. That, along with a lack of real commitment by Kodak's managers to the digital future, led to poor performance in digital products. Internally, Kodak's nascent digital unit had the status of an ugly stepchild. Yet the handwriting was clearly on the wall: electronic photography would replace film photography.

What spelled Kodak's death knell was the rise of the smartphone and cheap, good digital cameras. Film photography dominated the market right up until 2000. A few years later, film photography commenced a rapid decline. By the time Kodak filed for bankruptcy in 2012, digital photography was used more than 90 times as often as film; in that year, when roughly 380 billion digital photographs were shot, only 4 billion frames of still film were exposed.

This is the reality, too, of exponential growth curves. As Ray Kurzweil likes to point out, on an exponential curve, reaching a mere 1 percent adoption from 0.01 percent puts you halfway to 100 percent. With digital photography, as if someone had flipped on a light switch, suddenly the technology was better, cheaper, and more convenient. The demise of film—and of Kodak—was swift. Had Kodak understood that it was facing an exponentially growing product category, it might have met the challenge.

From Xerox, the original creator of the graphical user interface, to networking pioneer 3Com, to fast-fashion pioneer Forever 21, which declared bankruptcy in late 2019, the Hall of Toast is haunted by the ghosts of companies that once were hailed and later failed or shrank to a shadow of their former selves. As we were writing this book, the 170-year-old travel agency and travel-services company Thomas Cook, struggling to compete with Internet agencies, abruptly went bust, leaving thousands of travelers stranded and unable to return home.

Survival: An Endless Task

Staying out of the Hall of Toast is a never-ending task. Technology giant IBM started making office equipment, then smartly pivoted to computers, and then pivoted again to technology services and software, all under the guidance of legendary CEO Louis Gerstner. Gerstner initiated a formal process for creating innovative business at IBM, one that worked quite well, and IBM Life Sciences emerged from that rigorous process. But later managers dismantled Gerstner's business-innovation programs, and IBM has struggled to switch from technology services and the servers and boxed-software licenses in declining demand to cloud computing and other areas experiencing faster growth.

Facing multiple quarters of declining revenues, IBM responded by slashing its workforce. Even so, IBM is investing far less in necessary capital expenditures than its rivals are, and risks heading for the Hall of Toast—unless it makes another urgent course correction, which we hope it will.

Certainly, IBM's managers are aware of the risk. Under the guidance of new CEO Arvind Krishna and with the approval of outgoing CEO. Virginia Rometty, IBM made a "bet-the-company" acquisition in 2018, purchasing cloud computing and Linux giant Red Hat for $33 billion. This came after IBM had failed to internally jumpstart a viable cloud business, and after IBM's initial foray into A.I. with Watson resulted in lower revenues than anticipated and less in stalled technology progress in key sectors such as health care. Krishna is a very smart engineer, and the logic of the acquisition makes sense; but for IBM to truly avoid the Hall of Toast, the company will need to change its culture yet again to imbue the more nimble ethos of Red Hat and the faster metabolism of cloud computing into all it does.

Exponential trends can overwhelm even well-intentioned efforts to innovate. Gannett, the giant U.S. publisher of newspapers and operator of television stations, made strong efforts to innovate, but it has thus far failed to overcome the downdraft that has plagued both print-and, to a lesser degree, broadcast-advertising markets. Its share price having fallen 89 percent from its all-time peak in 2004, Gannett is in the process of merging with a cut-rate operator of media companies.[3] With the company that controls Gannett largely focusing on cost-cutting rather than on innovating to squeeze out more revenue, the one-time dominant force in the U.S. newspaper market, too, appears to be heading for the Hall of Toast.

Critical to understanding the forces consigning so many legacy leaders to oblivion is appreciating the effect of some recent disruptions in a range of key industries and even in government. In those disruptions lie the key insights for returning legacy companies to innovator status using the same techniques as the upstarts.

3

The Old Innovator's Dilemma versus the New Innovator's Dilemma

CHAPTER SUMMARY: This chapter provides an update to Clayton Christensen's insightful model of how companies experience and deal with innovation in a world in which disruption no longer comes only from bottom-up attacks and instead can come from any direction. We create a model, which we call the New Innovator's Dilemma, that explains this new reality, and then illustrate these omnidirectional disruptions in five sectors: media, retail, e-commerce and voice commerce, transportation and logistics, and finance. Then we dive into specific detail on some case studies: Amazon Go, Allbirds, and Tesla. Last, we study second-order disruptions in the context of the New Innovator's Dilemma.

When the late highly respected Harvard Business School professor Clayton Christensen published his best-selling book *The Innovator's Dilemma* in 1997,[1] the world was early in the digital explosion that accompanied the widespread adoption of the Internet. Christensen posited that good-enough technological innovation would allow startups to attack lower-end product categories in various market sectors.

The innovations would initially be inferior to incumbent processes and technology, leading legacy companies to dismiss the potential of the upstart firms and their technology; but inevitably, Christensen argued, the upstart firms and their technology would swim upstream and disrupt the entire industry over time by making goods of comparable or superior quality available at considerable cost savings.

Christensen found in his research that legacy companies were poorly equipped to adapt to disruptive innovations, for a variety of reasons, including the need to keep producing large revenues from existing products that would be cumbersome and risky to continually improve. He recommended that firms facing this sort of disruption open up a second company or create a separate branch, independent of the parent company. The new organization's task would be to create a competitor, grow the competitor, and ultimately cannibalize the parent company and allow the new subsidiary to continue capturing value for the original company and its shareholders.

This is surely an oversimplification of Christensen's original theory, which has been updated since. But *The Innovator's Dilemma* arose in a different technological epoch, and its prescriptions are themselves being disrupted by converging exponential technologies. Technology development and product adoption are occurring so much faster today than even a decade ago that the nature of the innovation game has changed radically. A host of compounding factors has created an entirely new innovator's dilemma game, one far more complex and difficult to navigate than the older scenario in which a new competitor making cheaper steel rebar and bottom-feeding on the least lucrative part of the market will swim upstream. And understanding the rules of this new innovation game is essential to playing it well.

Here are some of the most important ways in which the game has changed:

- The competition no longer comes from your industry alone; it may be, as Peter Diamandis once told me, two kids in a garage building an exponential technology.
- Innovation in a business model triumphs over innovation in products, and platforms triumph over business models.
- Companies that adopt technology sooner and more successfully gain an exponentially increasing advantage. Those that don't lead the disruptions become their casualties.
- The information now available has shifted power from seller to buyer; intellectual capital and brand no longer lock in the customer. You either build loyalty via value and innovation—or perish.
- The very nature of trust has changed. It was formerly institutions whose trust mattered; now it is individuals. A company's reputation rests on what an individual or community thinks of it, and ratings and reviews have become more important than brands and advertising.
- When it comes to management, command no longer works; management occurs through communication and persuasion.
- Innovation thrives in diversity, and it is your people who make it happen. These people, the "collective," can solve problems—or create them.
- Joining a startup rather than a large, established company is no longer regarded as risky; potential employees often perceive it as the fastest path to career advancement and the place for top performers.

The essential point of all these changes is that innovation is the key to business survival—innovation is a bottom-up process, not a top-down one. And underlying breakthrough innovation is the reality that everything that *can be* digitized *is being* digitized—and rapidly.

Improvements in computing have enabled first-order exponential infrastructure advancement in storage cost, network distribution and bandwidth, and sensor cost. With such improvements continuing, costs of all vectors are falling rapidly. For this reason, second-order disruptions are now being joined by third-order disruptions of the way systems fit together and of the way we interact with our technology.

Trust is a fine example. Public trust in systems such as Uber rests on our social recognition that online reputation systems can be effective; perhaps even more effective than legacy reputation systems. So we may feel in some ways more comfortable getting into a stranger's car than into a Yellow Cab, even though Yellow Cab is a brand that has been around for many decades and is a well-known quantity. These trust systems, such as Yelp and eBay, couldn't have evolved without the Internet, ubiquitous access, and social acclimatization to online trust.

All the changes that make second-order disruptions possible link directly or indirectly back to Moore's law and our rapid improvements in digital systems—and to the continuing pace of those improvements. As we look at the smartest companies that have taken advantage of these disruptive exponential advances, we see novel ways of approaching business with an eye to the future—even, in the case of Netflix, when the company's legacy business of renting DVDs appeared to be a lucrative standalone venture.

This brings us to what we'll call the *New* Innovator's Dilemma. Today, competition and disruption can come from anywhere: from below, from above, from adjacent fields, and from totally unrelated companies. Dollar Shave Club came literally out of nowhere, almost overnight; and Uber did not work from the bottom of the taxi market up, as Christensen's model dictates, but began as a way to call expensive limousines with a smartphone, pivoting to the mass market only after the company had attained a clear product-market fit. And Tesla began with an expensive sports car on par with a Ferrari and accessible to just as small a portion of the population.

Because innovation can come from any direction, legacy companies have to keep watch in all directions for upstarts.

The new diversity of attack vectors dictates that companies must have new strategies for dealing with disruption. Christensen's prescription was largely that, in order to counter a disruptive entrant coming from the bottom up, a legacy company should spin out a competing upstart free to compete from the bottom up. The New Innovator's Dilemma stipulates that competition can arrive suddenly and wallop higher-end, high-margin products, causing a more existential threat. In the span of a few years, the Apple Watch has cast doubt over the future of the market for independent fitness trackers (which, in part, is why leading fitness tracker Fitbit sold to Google after taking a battering on the public markets). No longer the mythical frog in the pot unnoticing of the water's rising temperature, legacy companies are the frog leaping about trying to understand how to respond to the boiling cupful of water from nowhere that has landed on its head.

One thing is clear: the pace of change and the breadth of innovation have pushed Innovators' Dilemmas new and old into entirely new territory.

From Netflix to Hulu to Cheddar and BuzzFeed: Massive Media Disruptions

When Netflix CEO and founder Reed Hastings decided to tackle the DVD business, he planned to use streaming media over the burgeoning broadband Internet to create an over-the-top (OTT) media service: a one-to-one relationship with customers. This ploy sought to take custom not only from Blockbuster (Netflix's rival) but also from large media organizations that controlled content production and the content-transmission pipes (cable and satellite television). Hastings knew, too, that the fate of his company depended on *net neutrality,* a legal principle that proscribes transmission companies' discrimination against content providers. It was, in part, this distribution plan that enabled Netflix to build a business that accounts for more than percent of global bandwidth consumption (which its subscribers pay for).[2]

Creating a streaming content behemoth was highly expensive. Netflix hired talented programmers by the dozen, many of them on seven-figure annual salary packages. The company became the largest consumer of cloud-computing capacity on Earth, paying tens and then hundreds of millions of dollars per annum. It had built the world's largest content-distribution company, without owning infrastructure and with minimal capital expenditures.

Hastings had rightly gambled that costs of bandwidth and cloud computing would continue to fall and that Netflix would benefit from that. Netflix was also taking a large gamble on the power of algorithms—code and software—to wring more efficiency out of bandwidth. In the face of the legacy media empires that had been built by installing many billions of dollars' worth of infrastructure—servers, data centers, and so on—Hastings's approach took vision and daring.

Of course, someone had to pay for the infrastructure that Netflix rented—and that was largely Jeff Bezos and Amazon, who first cracked the nut of rented computing on a massive scale. Amazon, one of the companies that best understands Moore's law, turned the business of selling partial chunks of computing into an incredible windfall of its own that has become the largest source of profits for the giant that Bezos built. Amazon used its negotiating power to obtain lower prices on ever-better technology even in areas less affected by the Moore's law trends, including storage, databases, bandwidth, SMS, email services, and nearly every other computation-dependent infrastructure capability that modern organizations depend upon.

The Fight for Attention and the Massive Shift in Valuations of Media Companies

In the footsteps of Netflix followed Hulu. Owned by a group of major content producers—including the United States' largest cable-television providers, Disney and Comcast—Hulu was designed to compete directly with Netflix, turning the tables on the upstart and enjoying all of the benefits in costs and distribution that Netflix did in order to grow so quickly. This was the revenge of the content studios (principally Disney and Comcast) and the owners of content-transmission pipes (including Comcast again), both of which Netflix had outwitted during its rapid rise. Hulu used a pure over-the-top media-service ploy, following Netflix's tactics to the letter, building an infrastructure in the cloud and seeking to access customers via broadband data connections that customers paid for as part of their monthly telecommunications bills rather than in traditional cable-television slots for which the content networks, such as HBO or ESPN, had to pay high slotting fees to companies such as Comcast.

What made this business model possible was laws preventing telecoms and cable companies from discriminating against content providers, enabling customers to use their allocated broadband as they saw fit for any service, including Netflix. The knowledge of how to build and run an extensive streaming video network had spread as the crew that had created Major League Baseball's excellent streaming capability in the United States began to outsource its expertise—and suddenly, in the late 2010s, every major content provider was striving to offer an OTT service of its own. The competition also included Google's YouTube, with its application YouTube TV, a strong and clear attack from an adjacent precinct of the media industry.

But perhaps the purest iterations of this media disruption arose from the new content upstarts such as BuzzFeed. Founded by MIT Media Lab alumnus Jonah Peretti, BuzzFeed sought to use social content's boundless replicability to attract participation and consumption. An unending stream of videos of the number of rubber bands required to burst a watermelon complemented listicles recycling trivia content, aiming to capture consumer attention and to keep it. BuzzFeed had taken brilliant advantage of its recognition that the modern Internet essentially was a vast marketplace for people's attention and that the catchiest offerings won—and it recognized specifically that the Internet had severely undermined the value of old-style journalism. A story painstakingly reported for months by an investigative reporter at a major legacy publication had become no more valuable economically than a copy-cat summary with no real reporting posted hastily by BuzzFeed (although much of the credit for this strategy goes to a previously founded publication, *The Huffington Post).*

Legacy publications railed against the practice as a form of theft. But BuzzFeed continued to expropriate "eyeball" time, and legacy media brands struggled to hold their readerships. Even today BuzzFeed remains far more valuable than many established media properties, as evident in the fire sale of Time, Inc. and once-prized properties such as *Fortune* and *Sports Illustrated.* (Nonetheless, BuzzFeed itself hired a team of journalists for original reporting, but it had to reduce the unit due to its unprofitability.)

And this brings us, ironically, to Cheddar. A video-programming startup launched by Jon Steinberg, who had served as the C.O.O. of BuzzFeed for four years, Cheddar strove to meld the cheap but engaging content style of BuzzFeed with the OTT video-programming strategy of Netflix and Hulu. Steinberg used the lessons of Hastings (Netflix) and Peretti (BuzzFeed) to spin up a mini-television and video empire. Reading the unbundling of content perfectly, Steinberg secured distribution deals with legacy cable-connected providers hungry for millennial content, simultaneously mounting a strong OTT campaign to sell directly to consumers. And Steinberg and Cheddar hit paydirt. Having founded the company in early 2016, Steinberg sold it for $200 million to Altice Media in the summer of 2019,[3] a whopping return after just three years for investors who had put just over $50 million into it, and a startling juxtaposition to long-established brands such as *BusinessWeek,* which sold for less than $5 million in cash.[4]

Retail Totally Disrupted: The Amazon Juggernaut (and Allbirds)

In October 2018, after more than 130 years in business, the iconic U.S. retailer Sears, Roebuck and Company filed for bankruptcy.[5] From modest beginnings as a mail-order vendor of watches direct to consumers, Sears had become the largest retailer in the United States. At bankruptcy, Sears was a shadow of its original self. The flagging retailer had struggled to adjust to the digital age and had found itself tied to decrepit stores in increasingly undesirable locations. Served by a revolving door of managers, Sears struggled to create a culture that would allow it to evolve and innovate out of its troubles, and a number of rejuvenation initiatives ultimately failed. On top of its poor locations, spotty service, and questionable product mix, Sears had found itself saddled with dated software systems that it had failed to upgrade. Constantly on a back foot, it had also found itself unable to take advantage of new personalization, delivery, or A.I. technologies and keep up with its retail competitors.

Yet even the demise of the country's formerly largest and most powerful retailer fits a common pattern. The 2010s have been a decade of turmoil in the retail industry, worldwide, with dozens of publicly traded retailers having failed. Other major retailers that have been struggling to grow, such as Gap stores, have closed hundreds of underperforming locations; and around the developed world, malls have closed, leaving behind empty hulks.

The pall at the mall has suited one giant player just fine. Amazon, the retail juggernaut, has precipitated the decimation of retail perhaps more than any other business. The increasing trend toward shopping online has rendered most physical locations (which function as distributed warehouses) expensive albatrosses, and traditional retailers have found themselves forced to compete in technology-intensive e-commerce. Amazon's meteoric rise is worth examining closely.

The tale of Amazon's rapid transformation from a bookstore into a technology giant and subsequently into an "everything" store offering hundreds of millions of items is well known. Beneath the surface, the layers of disruption it has engendered are staggering. Amazon has disrupted or is in the process of disrupting every important facet of retail commerce. Because it is so willing to invest large amounts of money in anticipation of longer-term returns, Amazon can take gambles that few others will. And it is doing so by making effective use of the radical technology breakthroughs now available to the world of business.

Online Commerce and Voice Commerce

In the United States, anywhere between 25 percent and 50 percent of all searches for products online begin either on Amazon.com or on Amazon's mobile app.[6] Despite Google's dominance in the field of search engines, Amazon has come to dominate product search. It does this with maniacal focus on making product search work well for customers. This shift is in its relatively early stages: growth of e-commerce continues to accelerate, at the cost of physical retail sales. Within Amazon's online product search, every element of the customer experience is analyzed in minute detail and tuned so finely that most product designers in the e-commerce realm hew closely to the Amazon method of building an online store.

Not only has Amazon built a dominant platform in the fastest-growing retail-sales medium, it has also become a major player in the realm of voice commerce—and Amazon has traditionally struggled with consumer electronics. The voice-assistance market has become the fastest-growing market in technology, and Amazon is in the lead with products powered by its Alexa voice assistant. Early research indicates too that Amazon skews voice-search results in favor of its own products (as it does in product searches on Amazon.com).[7]

Transportation and Logistics

By convincing hundreds of millions of customers to expect every purchase to arrive in two days or less, Amazon set a new norm in retail. Today, this norm is about to give way to an even more radical one: same-day delivery of most purchases. In the process, Amazon has disrupted the transportation and logistics segment that has become vital to retail. Its fleets of jets and trucks deliver from its dozens of distribution centers, and it offers logistics and distribution services to millions of other companies. In other words, Amazon is the largest logistics and transportation company most people don't know about. If we include its extended fleet of third-party delivery partners, it may even have become one of the largest five logistics and delivery companies in the world.

Amazon is also leading transformation in transportation: actively experimenting with drone delivery, an increasingly promising final-hop mode as battery energy density continues to improve and drone costs continue to fall.[8] In the United Kingdom, Australia, and the United States, drone delivery is likely to become legal and common within the next five years. This would potentially allow Amazon to completely own its supply chain, dispensing with the third-party final-hop delivery partners that are both a major expense and the source of its greatest uncertainty in the journey from warehouse to customer doorstep.

In its own warehouses, Amazon is among the leaders (which include its Chinese competitor Alibaba) in deploying robots to raise productivity, and has purchased several leading robotics startups, such as Kiva Systems, to cement its position. These robots are rapidly replacing human labor. For example, Amazon is using giant robotic arms to stack bins of goods and using low-set 300-pound wheeled robots to ferry stacks of bins around warehouse floors, in a dance choreographed for efficiency. Humans used to stack the bins and push the stacks; now they watch the robots and troubleshoot. Amazon's Staten Island facility, in New York City, is nearly 80,000 square meters in area; other Amazon facilities are larger still. No other major retailer outside China (with the exception of Walmart) has achieved a similar degree of automation on such a scale. In the one instance in which a competitor was bettering Amazon in warehousing, logistics, and automation—Diapers.com—Amazon bought the competitor.

Finance

Retail margins are traditionally thin, stretched by supply chains that demand advance payment for goods that consumers may not purchase for a full year. Amazon now offers loans and other financing to tens of thousands of merchants who do business on the site, often undercutting other financing options. What helps it do this well is its access to the sales performance of these vendors, which provides detailed insights into likely profit margins. It, too, has massive reams of data and insights into the detail, at every point in the supply chain, of how companies operate. And, because Amazon also manufactures its products for rebranding (and, in profitable categories, does so aggressively), it also knows how much each item should cost to make, enriching its insights into which vendors will warrant loans of what size and on what terms.

Amazon is not alone in the quest to break into the finance industry. Newer point-of-sale systems too, such as Square, offer credit on the basis of observable cash flow. A new generation of online-only, mobile-first banks, such as Monzo in the United Kingdom, has shown that providing a vastly superior customer experience at an unbeatable price can win wide adoption even in the most trust-sensitive industries—and even without physical branches.

A large clutch of insurance startups now seek to streamline a cumbersome legacy style of underwriting, using algorithms that can quickly access credit history, look at a phone image or a Google Earth photo, and study an applicant's online behavior in order to issue a policy in a matter of seconds. Western Union, the legacy provider of money-transfer services, is being challenged not only by now-entrenched new arrivals such as PayPal but also by even cheaper over-the-top companies such as TransferWise, which are forcing banks to drop some of their most lucrative and exorbitant legacy fees: their levies on wire transfers.

Amazon Go and Physical Stores

Any of the dozens of Amazon Go stores now springing up in chic districts of leading cities around the globe feel initially like an upscale convenience store or small market. A small number of staff members walk around offering help. One thing you won't need their help with is paying for your purchases. To enter the store, you need to launch your Amazon Go phone app; once it is running on your smartphone, you can walk out with any purchases you want to make, without even stopping at a register or a counter.

Of course, retail has been heading toward cashier-less stores and markets for many years, but Amazon Go's robotic functions pervade every aspect of its interactions with shoppers. Ubiquitous cameras capture every shopper activity, track eye motions, and guide restocking decisions, and Amazon will probably deploy its advanced facial-recognition capabilities in the future to eliminate even the need for a phone app; its key to your wallet, bank account, and credit card will be your face. Even now, each Amazon Go store is akin to a human-powered A.I. laboratory, connected back to Amazon's massive hive mind. Amazon Go, along with its Whole Foods grocery store chain, allows the company to finally close the loop between physical and online behaviors, giving it the most complete picture of buyer behavior that any company in history has enjoyed. Online and offline interaction inform each other for increasingly effective decisions.

Amazon Is Remaking All of Retail

Considering the areas in which Amazon is heavily investing in technology and innovation makes clear that the company is remaking the entire retail industry. This is causing all manner of disruption, as traditional retail struggles to adapt and to keep pace. None of this is to say that the smartest existing retailers can't compete and innovate, but competition with large, established firms is coming not only from the likes of Amazon but also from skyrocketing new startups. We touched on this with the story of Dollar Shave Club, which used a marketing innovation and a slightly tweaked business model—razors as a subscription service—to capture market share before legacy companies were able to react.

Another example of this, which is actually more Amazon-like, is the eyeglass maker Warby Parker. Selling a product that requires the human touch and a prescription and that is highly dependent on taste was considered, at the dawn of the broadband age, a nearly impossible feat. eBay brokered the sale, but primarily as a peer-to-peer marketplace for used and otherwise non-retail clothing, collectibles, and other items. Then the shoe company Zappos (which, unsurprisingly, Amazon later acquired) was one of the early companies to break into high-touch online retail. Warby not only conquered high touch but also rolled out physical stores, financed by its online presence. Those stores log some of the highest sales turnover per square foot of any physical operation.[9] (The lead among non-luxury retailers is generally held by Apple.) More impressive still, the pace of development of these upstart retailers is accelerating, via the same trends in technology, business, and consumption that we mentioned in the previous section.

Allbirds: From Zero to $1 Billion in Two Years

The idea seems almost too silly to be true: a comfortable pair of wool sneakers made with advanced fabric technologies and eco-friendly sugarcane foam and favored by elitist venture capitalists and startup founders becomes a billion-dollar company in a few short years. Yet that precisely describes the trajectory of Allbirds, a San Francisco apparel startup that, like Dollar Shave Club, grew rapidly by marketing expertly and directly to customers. Allbirds had something more: a technologically differentiated shoe that resisted odor and was insanely comfortable. The company wove its woolen uppers onto a unique type of foam made from sugarcane residue, creating a near-zero-carbon footprint. And, altruistically, Allbirds published its foam recipe.

First a darling of the tech set, Allbirds went mainstream quickly, selling the vast majority of its product via its own website. As Warby Parker did, Allbirds eventually set up a select group of physical outlets in high-traffic parts of luxury city neighborhoods. Ironically, Allbirds grew so popular that it attracted the attention of none other than Amazon, which pushed out a copycat product in September 2019.

Allbirds combines many elements of earlier successful startups in high-touch products, such as Zappos (with free shoe delivery and return), Warby, Bonobos, and others. Allbirds wove together an innovative product with rapid and effective marketing, using legacy distribution methods to crack massive but staid markets.

The significant difference between the results of the two is most obvious in the pace of disruption: managing to create an entirely new niche, Allbirds disrupted the footwear market in a mere two years.

Because creating vertically integrated retail companies without massive capital outlays is now much easier than ever before, an Allbirds, unlike legacy shoe companies, has a much faster cash-conversion cycle, spending far less time waiting for cash to roll in. Consequently, it does not need to create seasonal collections but can move at its own (faster) pace.

In retail, the "fast fashion" category has been one of comparative growth for a long time; Gap's Old Navy brand is so much more successful than its sister brands that the company has considered carving out the subsidiary as a separate entity and taking it public. But Allbirds exemplifies how quickly startups from anywhere can capture market share.

Tesla Cars as Software and the Art of the Impossible

After no more than a decade in production, Teslas are the best-selling electric vehicles on the planet. In 2018, Tesla outstripped not only all other automotive brands but also all automotive groups, with delivery of 245,240 units and a 12 percent market share in the plug-in allelectric segment. Tesla's U.S. unit sales had skyrocketed from 48,000 in 2017 to 182,400 in 2018. Reviewers had lavished praise on Teslas, and the new vehicles had garnered glowing safety ratings. Tesla is a prime case of what happens when a car company chooses to behave like a customer-focused software company such as Apple, which has legendarily charged high fees for a combination of beautiful hardware and slick software. Part of Tesla's legend is the special acceleration mode, in one of its models, that endows the vehicle with a time from zero to 60 mph of less than 2.3 seconds, the fastest ever recorded by a production vehicle.[10] CEO Elon Musk hilariously named it Ludicrous Mode. And who wouldn't want to buy a car capable of a Ludicrous Mode?

In fact, Musk has shaken up the car world by thinking very, very differently and betting on a host of exponential trends that he believes will make Tesla better able to undertake second-order innovation. For starters, Tesla behaves as if a car were a software product that happened to have a skin and seats, rather than vice versa. To be sure, all of today's cars are software intensive: the average vehicle contains millions of lines of computer code, controlling a host of key systems and onboard computers. But Tesla has, at Musk's urging, fully embraced the software ethos. It ships frequent software updates to its cars, improving performance and safety constantly. Ludicrous Mode, too, was a software update—and a delightful surprise that led many commentators to compare the speedy software upgrade to "Easter eggs" (surprise gifts or revelations) in video games.

Basing automobile systems squarely in software capable of updates has many benefits: speed, flexibility, and the ability to add new features far more swiftly and easily. Then there is safety, which brings us to Tesla's unique way of taking advantage of A.I. As noted previously, Tesla treats its cars as an intelligent network. The company constantly collects data from cars on the road, using them both to improve vehicle performance and, more famously, to power the machine-learning systems that will be necessary for driverless cars, and it has the largest library of vehicle road data from which to build autonomous vehicle systems. This is not to say that other car makers are not gathering data; but Tesla built its technology infrastructure to be always on and always in touch with its vehicles, with A.I. central to the company's strategy.

A third Tesla innovation concerns batteries. This is nearer a linear than an exponential innovation, but it is illustrative of Musk's thinking. To ensure an ample supply of batteries (one of the elements required for batteries, lithium, being in short supply) at good prices, Tesla decided to build the Gigafactory—one of the world's largest battery factories. Tesla calculated that mainstream acceptance of its cars would necessitate pricing them at or below comparable internal-combustion vehicles, and that—batteries being the costliest item in driverless cars—battery prices would have to fall. Relying on its own battery factory also gives Tesla much more control over its fate; nearly all other car makers are ordering batteries from third parties.

Tesla's ultimate vision is far from realized. Musk has been open about viewing Tesla as a Trojan Horse to remake the world's energy supply and radically shift our energy sources to renewable ones. Tesla's home-battery business, which dovetails nicely with the Gigafactory, and Tesla's solar-panel business (which has been flagging of late)[11] hitch Tesla's fortunes to a runaway exponential freight train: the plummeting costs of solar power panels. In a way, too, Tesla's trajectory illustrates how innovation and competition can arise from adjacent fields. Tesla is, at heart, less an automobile manufacturer than an interloper from the software ecosystem, with very little car DNA in its workforce.

To say Tesla is already successful may be premature. The company remains heavily in debt, with many short-selling investors betting that it will have to raise more money and pay a hefty price for it—though so far it is these investors who have paid the price for betting against Musk. But Tesla has single-handedly brightened global perceptions of electric cars, doing what dozens of companies have tried but failed to do—and has thereby induced the world's automotive giants to accelerate their plans for electrics and to invest in autonomous vehicles, in the same way that SpaceX forced the large satellite-launch providers to rethink their legacy approaches to building rockets and boosting satellites into orbit.

The Second-Order Innovator's Dilemma

A close look at the examples we've provided of industry disruptors—Netflix, Amazon, Tesla—reveals that none of them actually meet the criteria for a classic Christensen Innovator's Dilemma analysis. Tesla entered the market with a very high-end product: its first Roadster is now a collector's item. The Roadster sold for about $100,000 when it was first released; Tesla has swum downstream since then, and is only now entering the lower end of the vehicle market. Nor did Amazon work from the bottom up: it took a systems-thinking approach and applied it broadly to one industry after another to improve all aspects of that industry. In a sense, what Amazon employed was more an innovative way of *thinking* about business than an innovative business.

Netflix and the OTT content providers have certainly undercut the costs of legacy cable and pay TV providers; and, of the three, Netflix bears the most resemblance to a classic Innovator's Dilemma case study. In reality, a technology company masquerading as a content company,

Netflix invested heavily in content-delivery technologies using its video-delivery expertise, and in using A.I. to automatically recommend further viewing at the end of every viewing program. This is not bottom up; it is a revolutionary way of engaging with users on a variety of devices, of building an enormous infrastructure on a subscription basis alone. To compare Netflix's strategy to those of startup manufacturers of steel rebar does the innovative company no justice. In other words, very clearly, the rules of the innovation game have changed. In the next chapter, we will study why legacy companies fail and what company innovation now hinges on.

PART II

Why Top-Down Innovation Efforts Usually Fail

In the pre-exponential era, although many companies met their demise through competitors' bottom-up innovation, such incursions almost always came from within their industry and were, as Clayton Christensen documented, frontal assaults. In the exponential era, as we've noted, with the world changing in myriad ways, legacy companies can fail for many other reasons.

What's more, a company can fail much faster today: competition is fiercer and wider, technology is changing faster, starting a company even in a capital-intensive industry is less expensive, and customer tastes are more fluid—all leaving legacy companies without the luxury of time in which to figure out how to more effectively compete against startups. This is why, as we noted in the previous section, the turnover in the Dow Jones Industrials is rapidly accelerating and even companies once noted as innovators are struggling to keep pace with others.

Rapid innovation requires care in its coordination, as apparent in the recent fate of Boeing and its 737 Max, which exhibited a chain of cascading failures that led to the loss of hundreds of lives when fear of losing market share drove the company to move faster without creating systems to ensure safety in sustaining this accelerated development.[1]

Equally challenging to legacy companies is the concentration of power deriving from technological superiority and, similarly, from willingness to deploy the latest technology earlier and in more-important roles than ever before. Economists have noted, in industry after industry, rapid profit consolidations by smaller groups of world-beating companies. In some cases, such as that of the financial industry, this may be due to regulatory capture. But in many others, it is a natural effect of companies' proving better at harnessing the power of what Erik Brynolfson and Andrew McAfee call *the second machine age.* They write: "Computers and other digital advances are doing for mental power—the ability to use our brains to understand and shape our environments—what the steam engine and its descendants did for muscle power."[2] In the first machine age, the original Industrial Revolution, companies took decades to understand how to reconfigure their factories to better adapt machinery to new power sources rather than earlier sources such as waterwheels.

For example, factories designed to harness waterpower tended to be vertically stacked, as this was the reality of collecting power from a slowly spinning wheel. Over time, as the steam engine and later electricity allowed power to be distributed more evenly across a factory floor, factory owners created layouts that eliminated the need for vertical travel. The ultimate expression of this optimization, of course, was Henry Ford's moving assembly line, which slashed the time required to assemble an automobile from nearly half a day to less than two hours.

Even perception of the possibility of such shifts was a painful process of exploration and of trial and error. But the early victors reaped massive spoils as a result of their fundamentally better grasp of how to use the technological shifts of the first industrial age to implement their vision of the world, which allowed them to create enormously profitable manufacturing juggernauts. We are probably seeing a similar dynamic in the second industrial age, as the more technologically proficient companies improve their ability to harness exponentially advancing technologies to accelerate their businesses and generate outsized profits (which, by the way, allow them to pay more for the best talent).

Such proficiency is more difficult to maintain now than it used to be. In most of Christensen's Innovator's Dilemma examples, a single innovation provided the dilemma, and the incumbents could clearly see the innovation's threat (though they often decided to ignore it because it was too far down market to affect their profits). Today, though, the dilemma arises from the fact of multiple exponentially advancing technologies combining.

So yes: we have learned a great deal about innovation since Christensen first brought his concept to the world, and in this section, we analyze and debunk a host of common assumptions about innovation. We then further discuss common failure modes that sink companies, and we attempt to explain them through the lens of modern technologies and altered social and communication structures.

4

False Assumptions, Broken Models, Wasted Effort

CHAPTER SUMMARY: This chapter looks at the failed strategies and tactics that organizations have used to try to systematize and foster applied and organic innovation, including innovation clusters, Silicon Valley outposts, and dedicated corporate innovation teams. We examine why all these strategies have failed, and why it has been so hard to replicate the magic of Silicon Valley.

Some readers will recall the halcyon innovation days of the 1990s, when everything seemed possible and governments invented various strategies to spur innovation in entire cities. Remember the announcements about science parks and Silicon Valley-like tech hubs that they called industry clusters? Alas, most of those triumphant ideas have been debunked, and most of the attempts to spark top-down innovation fashion have quietly fizzled.

There are important lessons for businesses and governments to learn from these failures. Development of innovation centers is and always will be organic, from the bottom up. And though business executives love to have them, corporate Silicon Valley outposts are boondoggles: innovation by osmosis doesn't work very well, partly because the outposts—treated as shiny baubles rather than core parts of product development—are removed from the company and do not tend to face the same pressures to survive and thrive.

Corporate innovation centers, too, fail most of the time. Assigning innovation to parts of an organization limits possibilities and corporate buy-in and creates useless innovation bubbles. More broadly, increasing research and development (R&D) spending in a vacuum or even with a relatively strong plan tends not to work: there has been no clear correlation between levels of R&D budget and corporate performance. Money alone can neither buy innovation nor change corporate culture to become more innovative and faster moving.

On the other hand, we have strong evidence that creating an innovation culture, or a culture that encourages and prizes key precursors to innovation, will generate improvements. It is all about focusing on your people. And doing that doesn't cost an arm and a leg. The last section of this chapter will allude to the effect of culture, which we will address in greater detail later in the book.

The Failure of Industry Clusters

By the 1960s, Silicon Valley had already cemented its position as the world's preeminent technology center. The Valley commenced its journey with the commercialization of the electronics industry, establishing key industry-academic partnerships that generated a positive feedback loop between nearby Stanford University and the high-tech Valley companies. French president Charles de Gaulle visited the Valley and was impressed by its sprawling research parks, set amid farms and orchards south of San Francisco.

Figure 4.1 Gordon Moore (left) and Robert Noyce in 1970, having founded Intel in 1968 when they left Fairchild Semiconductor.
Image Credit: Intel Free Press

Classic Cluster

The early team at Fairchild Semiconductor, in San Jose, California, made the first integrated circuit, from silicon. Two of the team's members, Gordon Moore and Robert Noyce (pictured in Figure 4.1), went on to found Intel.

Stanford had already given birth to successful companies, including Hewlett-Packard (HP), Varian Associates, Watkins-Johnson, and Applied Technologies. (HP, of course, went on to become an iconic brand, and remains in existence two decades into the 21st century.)

These companies expanded the frontiers of technology, and from them came more companies, which focused on building innovations and symbiotic relationships. The resultant networks laid the conceptual foundations for the largest assembly line of technology powerhouses—and arguably the largest amount of corporate wealth creation—ever witnessed. Something unusual was happening here, in both innovation and entrepreneurship.

Unsurprisingly, other regions recognized Silicon Valley's success and attempted to replicate its dynamics. The first significant attempt to re-create Silicon Valley emerged from a consortium of high-tech companies in New Jersey in the mid-1960s (though it should be noted that the Radio Corporation of America and its offshoot the David Sarnoff Research Center, founded in New Jersey, were innovation engines pre-dating the Valley by decades).

The New Jersey consortium recruited Frederick Terman, who was retiring from Stanford having served there as provost, professor, and engineering dean. Sometimes called the "father of Silicon Valley," Terman had transformed Stanford's young engineering school into an innovation juggernaut. By encouraging science and engineering departments to cooperate closely, linking them to nearby entrepreneurs and like-minded companies, and tightly focusing applied research on solving industry problems, Terman had created a culture of cooperation and information exchange that quickly took root and today still defines and shapes Silicon Valley.

New Jersey wanted to clone that dynamic and its powerful outcome. The Garden State was already a leading high-tech center: it was home to the laboratories of 725 companies, including RCA, Merck, and Bell Labs. It boasted a science and engineering workforce of roughly 50,000; but, with no prestigious engineering university in the area, New Jersey companies had to look outside for recruits. This was before the rise of New York University, Rockefeller University, and the various state universities of New York as research powerhouses. And even though

Princeton University was nearby, its faculty back then mostly avoided applied research or close associations with industry. (Oddly though, making atomic weapons for the government was fine.) So, led by the top management at Bell Labs, New Jersey's business and government leaders charged Terman with building a university that resembled Stanford.

Terman created a plan to accomplish that, but he was unable to obtain the consensus necessary to enact it—because, curiously, the very industry seeking this change wouldn't and couldn't collaborate in it. As documented by Stuart W. Leslie and Robert H. Kargon in a 1996 paper titled "Selling Silicon Valley," RCA would not sign a partnership with Bell Labs; Esso elected not to embed its best researchers into a university; and drug firms such as Merck preferred to keep their research dollars in house.[1] Even though they knew that working together would make them all better in the long run, companies refused to work with competitors.

Terman attempted a similar plan in Dallas. He failed there too, for similar reasons.

Later, the renowned Harvard Business School professor Michael Porter proposed a different method of creating regional innovation centers. Rather than rely on corporate cooperation, Porter proposed tapping existing research universities. His simple observation—not a novel one—was that geographic concentrations of interconnected companies and specialized suppliers offered knowledge-intensive industries productivity and cost advantages. In addition, the collective bubbling intellectual capital would, he posited, spur the creation of new firms. Porter postulated that in mixing these ingredients, as in adding ingredients to a pot of soup, regions could create clusters of innovation.[2]

Porter and legions of consultants espousing this methodology installed top-down clusters for governments all over the world. The formula was always the same: pick a hot industry, build a science or innovation park next to a research university, provide subsidies and incentives for the chosen industries (say, biotech or semiconductor research) to locate there, and seek a pool of venture capital.

It was an innovation catastrophe.

Sadly, the soup never came to a boil—anywhere. Hundreds of regions all over the world collectively spent tens of billions of dollars trying to build small, top-down replicas of Silicon Valley. We cannot cite a single success that is truly self-sustaining and innovative in the way that Silicon Valley is innovative. It was easy to identify the ingredients for innovation. As it turns out, however, the recipe was less obvious.

What Porter and Terman failed to realize was that neither academia, industry, nor even the U.S. government's funding for military research into aerospace and electronics was a key catalyst in creating Silicon Valley; rather, it was the people and the relationships that Terman had so carefully fostered among Stanford faculty and industry leaders. That painstaking and non-transactional process had yielded immense and self-propagating social and intellectual capital that has maintained dominance over global innovation for nearly 50 years.

The Missing Ingredients: Culture, People, and Genuine Connection

University of California, Berkeley, professor AnnaLee Saxenian has cogently exposed the importance of culture, people, and connections in building innovation. Her 1994 book *Regional Advantage: Culture and Competition in Silicon Valley* insightfully compared the evolution of Silicon Valley with that of Route 128—the highway ring around Boston—to explain why no region has been able to replicate the California success story.[3]

Saxenian explained that, until the 1970s, Boston was significantly ahead of Silicon Valley in startup activity and venture-capital investments. The region had birthed numerous important technology companies in that era, including Digital Equipment Corporation

(DEC), one of the most powerful and profitable computer companies of its day, and Wang Laboratories. In fact, Route 128 had a real information-concentration advantage because of its proximity to East Coast industrial centers. Silicon Valley was closer than that to some aerospace production in Southern California, but the sheer volume of nearby industrial activity was much greater on the East Coast and the near Midwest during that era.

Despite Boston's head start, by the 1980s, Silicon Valley and Route 128 looked alike: a mix of large and small tech firms, world-class universities, venture capitalists, and military funding. And then Silicon Valley raced ahead and left Route 128 in the dust. Today, Boston remains a distant second in receipt of venture-capital funding, in the value of companies created, and in total job creation from venture-backed companies: one metric that many accept as a relatively strong proxy for innovation.

The factors that let Silicon Valley outshine Route 128 were, at root, cultural. Silicon Valley experienced high rates of job-hopping and company formation. The professional networks and easy information exchange were more fluid and accepted. These soft traits lent the Valley advantages. Valley firms understood that collaborating and competing at the same time led to success. This even showed up in state laws: California barred noncompetition agreements, discouraging litigation against former employees. (For this reason, many of the world's largest hedge funds and financial institutions to this day refuse to employ knowledge workers in California—revealing much about those institutions and their views on innovation!)

The Power of an Open System That Welcomes Outsiders

The Valley's novel ecosystem supported experimentation, risk-taking, and sharing of the lessons of success and failure. More explicitly, Silicon Valley was an open system—a thriving, real-world social network that existed long before Facebook. To be clear, throughout history we have seen similar roots of innovation. Holland shared many of these traits during the centuries in which the Netherlands—a small, waterlogged country with a small population—was responsible for an astounding number of innovations and a wildly disproportionate share of global economic activity. Long before the Valley, Holland was a social network that rewarded risks and thrived on the open movement of ideas and people. Holland also shared another trait with Silicon Valley: openness to other ways of life and other cultures. Because it was happy to accept and embrace without conditions the best and the brightest people, Silicon Valley became a magnet for global talent.

From 1995 to 2005, 52.4 percent of engineering and technology startups in Silicon Valley had one or more founders born outside the United States, according to research conducted by Vivek at Duke University with the help of AnnaLee Saxenian of UC Berkeley.[4] That was twice the rate seen in the United States as a whole. Immigrants such as Vivek who came to Silicon Valley found it easy to adapt and assimilate. The rules of engagement were openly shared, and the Valley's inhabitants both participate in existing networks and create their own networks. (For South Asians, for example, The Indus Entrepreneurs, or TiE, grew to become a powerful sub-network within the broader Silicon Valley context.)

You read about the PayPal Mafia or the diaspora of early Apple engineers who went on to form their own successes. These networks cross-pollinated or merged as convenient, as did for example Tony Fadell, one of the key designers and product minds behind the iPod, in founding the home-thermostat company Nest, which Apple's rival Google acquired for $3.2 billion.[5]

Equally important, in this network, all participate as relative equals. Yes, a founder who sold a company for a billion dollars or an engineer with a pedigree from storied Valley firms has a leg up in starting companies. But it is absolutely the case that dreamers with a paper napkin for a business plan can still get an audience with some of the smartest and most powerful people in Silicon Valley if they are persistent, polite, and persuasive.

This freedom to form relationships and share ideas is, more than anything else, what innovation requires. The understanding of global markets that immigrants bring with them, their knowledge of different disciplines, and the links that they provide to their home countries have given the Valley an unassailable competitive advantage as it has evolved from making radios and computer chips to producing search engines, social media, medical devices, and clean-energy technology.

The Valley is a meritocracy that is, however, far from perfect. And some of its flaws tear at the very fabric that makes it unique. First, women and certain minorities, such as blacks and Hispanics, are largely absent from the ranks of company founders and boards despite diversity's having become a top priority for all Valley companies and venture capitalists. This is likely to be a barrier to the Valley's further growth and has probably motivated it to focus on certain types of problems and ignore others. (Biotech and pharma startups focusing on women's health and conditions that disproportionately affect people of African descent, for example, have consistently been shortchanged.)

In addition, venture capitalists have a herd mentality and largely fund startups that produce short-term results—leading to a preponderance of social media, advertising-technology, and blockchain apps.

Also problematic is that the Valley environment values money so highly that even top venture capitalists are willing to overlook repugnant behavior and toxic corporate leadership, both of which we witnessed for years throughout the growth of the ride-hailing company Uber and in the medical-technology company Theranos (where a culture of dishonesty was repeatedly called out but consistently ignored).

Finally, real-estate prices and home-rental rates are so high that most Americans (or people from any other country) can't afford to relocate there, so it is becoming harder to maintain the open flow of people, the Valley's lifeblood.

Though real and serious, these challenges arise only because of the Valley's success and power. No one cares about trying to save an isolated regional innovation cluster that spent hundreds of millions of hard-earned state subsidies in vain to build an innovation engine. And few people believe, anymore, that you can impose innovation from the top down as a regional cluster. It's a bankrupt idea. Yet, like a zombie, it continues to play out as a slow-motion failure all over the world. In 2012, the Monitor Group filed for bankruptcy, saddled with debts and unable to pay its bills. This high-powered consulting group had once been one of the loudest proponents of industry clusters—and its founder was none other than Harvard Business School professor Michael Porter.

Silicon Valley Outposts: Boondoggles and Junkets

The property at 3521 Hillview Avenue sits in the middle of Silicon Valley history. A stone's throw from the Xerox Palo Alto Research Center (PARC), which birthed so many early technology innovations, and a five-minute drive (or bike ride) from the campus of Stanford University, the beautiful glass building, tucked into a quiet street, is the Valley outpost of the Ford Motor Company. Dubbed Ford Greenfield Labs, the facility houses hundreds of Ford workers—and, in many respects, the future aspirations of Ford. There, engineers from Stanford and Apple work on autonomous vehicles, new ways to use sensors, and other cutting-edge concepts that Ford believes it will need in order to effectively compete in the uncertain future of the transportation industry.

There are nearly a thousand corporate outposts in Silicon Valley, in a number of flavors, few of them successful. Corporate venture funds invest in startups. Corporate incubators provide office space and mentors in order to develop solutions to the corporation's problems. Corporate accelerators provide seed funding and support intrapreneurs within corporations. Corporate partnerships occupy corporate business-development offices. And, finally, there are specialized R&D centers such as Ford Greenfield Labs to attract local technology talent and, ideally, transfer some of their expertise back to the corporations.

This setup totals billions of dollars each year in annual expenditures and investments. And the rationale is laudable. In the case of Ford, the perceived threat to the company's future is real. Autonomous vehicle technology is advancing quickly inside tech companies (such as Google and Apple) that in 2010 would not have registered as possible competitors. Google has the early data lead, with its Waymo division logging a vast advantage in the total vehicle-mileage of its driverless cars. As we mentioned earlier in this book, in an era of exponential competition, threats can readily arise from totally unrelated companies seeking to crack new markets.

Ford's reaction—opening a lab to immerse itself in the action—is common. Unfortunately, the history of setting up corporate outposts close to the innovation action has shown few successes. But this has not prevented hundreds of major companies from setting up shop in Silicon Valley in one form or another, ranging from full-blown labs to R&D centers such as that of Ford (and many other automakers).

The Reasons for Outposts' Failures

There are many reasons for the failure of these well-intentioned forays.

Lack of Real Commitment

For starters, there's the element of commitment. For the most part, these outposts are helmed by executives or promising young employees from the corporate mothership who struggle to "get" the culture of the Valley. They arrive with good remuneration packages, few ties, and a loose charter to "help the company understand what's happening." A

Silicon Valley outpost is rarely held to a specific goal, and even when it is, accountability tends to be fluid. This is a major problem, as it makes the outpost nothing more than a junket and fact-finding mission with little real output or rationale.

Isolation from the Mothership

In addition, these outposts tend to be isolated from their mothership. Most outposts are several time zones, if not a continent, away from their main company, loosening even their temporal bonds. This distance results in less contact and in mutual unawareness. And, because there is no formal way to transmit information back to the mothership, even if the occupants of the outpost are diligent and manage to understand the Valley, the information they capture and the social capital they gain is hard to transfer home.

Best Employees Are Hired Away

The outposters also realize that their outpost is always a tenuous line item, subject to cuts whenever the mothership experiences deterioration in its balance sheet or merely a change in leadership. It is, in the parlance of Wall Street, a "non-core asset." So the best outpost employees tend to get hired away by smart startups or by legacy technology players who recognize their value well before their mother corporation understands it. And the worst of them view their posting as a plum gig in an awesome part of the world that they can use as an innovation credential for their next stop on the corporate merry-go-round.

In a nutshell, the outpost arrivals—both individual and organizational—are not necessarily in Silicon Valley for the long haul.

The Antithesis of the Valley Ethos

Such mutual uncertainty is antithetical to the attitude and approach that have made the Valley successful and that allow new entrants to thrive: a clear commitment to long-term participation and contribution.

None of this is to say that the outposters' intentions are bad or that the mothership is unjustified in wanting a piece of the Valley. But just showing up—even with a specific idea in mind—doesn't enable innovation.

Hiring Valley Leaders Doesn't Work, Either

Another approach is to hire existing Valley leaders and talent to staff an outpost. The theory is that they will bring over their networks and values and enable the company to take advantage of their social and intellectual capital. In reality, though, corporate headquarters are generally reluctant to devolve much true authority and autonomy to their outposts, which instead assume largely consultative roles.

This outpost is unable to provide more than an R&D capacity hard to obtain elsewhere. Silicon Valley is home to many more autonomous-vehicle engineers than is Detroit—but they are not coming from an automotive background. So these imported outpost leaders almost always depart, frustrated, to return to one of the big tech companies whence they came. The sad reality is that the top talent does not want to work for legacy corporations.

Inability to Match Tech Companies' Compensation Packages

What's more, legacy corporations can't match the compensation packages that the leading technology companies offer. So either they hire short-timers who may be very good but are taking it easy for a bit in a corporate gig, or they hire those who have been unable to stay at Google, Apple, and other leading organizations.

Inability to Solve Real Problems because of Disconnection from Real Customers

More fundamentally, though, corporate outposts do not solve the sponsoring organization's core problems, and they remain disconnected from the organization's customers and corporate needs. Residents of an outpost will continue to receive the emails and slide decks and will continue to sit in on the all-hands phone calls. But, because they are no longer talking to customers or the sales team or others on the front line, outposters lose touch with the true needs and wants of the customers.

Moreover, most Silicon Valley outposts are—as are outposts anywhere—too small in scale to drive real disruption and innovation. This is underscored by the tendency of outpost employees to do things in the same way they are done in their legacy corporation: with little passion or sense of urgency, and with a heavy reliance on specialization and multiple departments.

Venture Capital Spreading More Broadly

Another important consideration is that, over time, venture capital and innovation have begun to spread more broadly. Stockholm, Beijing, London, and New York all host thriving innovation ecosystems. China has created a powerful circular innovation engine by working with Chinese nationals who are educated in the United States and Canada and who return to China to work in engineering or research roles in their country of birth. China is now the fastest-growing pool of venture-backed startups and is racing ahead in innovation.

So, although each innovation ecosystem has followed its own path to some degree, their commonalities mirror the development path of Silicon Valley, and their common ethos is more similar than dissimilar to Silicon Valley's. And all of those successes are long-term projects that, far from relying upon osmosis, result from painstaking reciprocal, non-transactional relationship building: the creation of a valuable social network that cannot be replicated or mocked up merely by renting some prime real estate in a hot location and airdropping in a team from the mothership.

Ford Labs Was Not Enough

In the end, Ford realized that Greenfield Labs was not going to solve its problems of navigating the new challenges of mobility and transportation. The labs remained, but the company also decided to invest billions of dollars in a slate of well-regarded autonomous transportation startups, including Argo and Rivian. We'll discuss later why this invest-in-the-best strategy, executed properly, outperforms an innovation outpost in terms of corporate innovation.

The Folly of Dedicated Top-Down Corporate Innovation Teams

Companies with a long track record of innovation usually bend over backward to include everyone as a potential innovator. Many large companies, though, attempt—often at the behest of corporate consultants—to spur innovation by creating an internal innovation team. Generally comprising stellar employees who excel at climbing the corporate ladder (many of whom have obtained an innovation credential from an association of innovation professionals in order to become "innovation experts") and tell the company what works and what doesn't, the innovation team's mandate is usually to seek innovation and bring the best on offer into the company.

Sometimes corporate innovation teams look to bring in startups as partners. Sometimes they work with their companies' venture-capital arms seeking strategic investments in startups that could be disruptive in their industries. Many corporate innovation teams oversee internal startup competitions and funds, and often serve on committees to judge startup performance and allocate their next funding round among them.

A separate location is usual for the internal innovation team and internal startups—which, as this chapter has illustrated, all too often results in an innovation black hole, albeit one with bright colors and bean bags strewn about.

All these tendencies can, and usually do, create counterproductive incentives, bogging down corporate innovation by poisoning innovation efforts. As do those in corporate outposts, innovation teams struggle to identify, let alone focus on, customer problems. Without real power to make things happen, and without real budgets, they turn over quickly, because their most perceptive members realize that this is not an effective way to enact change in a company. Thus do the vast majority of corporate innovation efforts—more than 90 percent, according to one study by the consultancy Capgemini and Altimeter Group—fail.[6]

Innovation Teams Can't See New Business Models

The biggest problem that all these flavors of canned innovation face is one of recognizing a change in business model. Changing a business model is far more painful and harder to comprehend than bringing in a new technology. This is why it takes a radical startup such as Lyft or Uber to bring something that is head-smackingly obvious into the light, such as the concept of attaching demand to supply for transportation via smartphones. It's why almost all of the legacy I.T. giants (Microsoft being an exception), including Oracle and IBM, are struggling to compete in a world of cloud computing in which server space is divided into smaller and smaller pieces and sold off by the hour or by the minute—and in which a simple move such as attaching a mail-order option and turning razor blade sales into a subscription business can enable a small startup to snatch 10 percent of the multi-billion-dollar North American market for men's shaving products.

Innovation Teams Struggle to Identify Nascent Markets

The famed venture capitalist Marc Andreessen is best-known for his visionary op-ed in the *Wall Street Journal* titled "Why Software Is

Eating the World." But those who follow him closely also know that Andreessen feels that software alone is not sufficient to eat the world and grow giant companies. In a less-famous blog post, Andreessen states his opinion that neither the quality of the team nor the quality of the product matters nearly as much as market demand for the innovation's projected benefits. "In a great market—a market with lots of real potential customers—the market pulls product out of the startup. The market needs to be fulfilled and the market will be fulfilled, by the first viable product that comes along," Andreessen wrote in a post titled "The Only Thing That Matters."[7]

Corporate innovation teams struggle mightily to supply these nascent markets, because they cannot walk a mile in the shoes of their customers. Judging or generating ideas for others to execute is a poor vantage point from which to see opportunities for market innovations that lead to successful products. For that, you need an evangelical zeal that can come only from a true founder mentality and a true emotional buy-in and commitment to the process of building something from nothing.

We have covered some of the ways in which innovation efforts have failed. Industry clusters can't be readily engineered and tend to sputter out: while a Silicon Valley outpost offers an alluring prospect of bellying up to the beasts of innovation, osmosis is a weak force for absorbing innovation culture, let alone transplanting it into an organization that is struggling to reinvent itself. Likewise, corporate innovation teams tend to fail because they are top down, set apart from the rest of the company, and trapped in an ivory tower disconnected from reality. Bad ideas follow, money is wasted, and innovation gets lost in the shuffle.

5

The Rules of the Game Have Changed in Critical Ways

CHAPTER SUMMARY: This chapter covers many of the social and technological changes retain underlying success and failure in business today, including changes in communication, changes in market dynamics and power, changes in the role of community in company formation and growth, and the increasing role that "open" business models are playing in the global economy.

Xiaomi is the biggest smartphone maker that no one seems to know about. In China, Xiaomi shot from obscurity to become the nation's largest maker of smartphones in less than a decade. Often criticized as an Apple copycat, Xiaomi produced slick phones with beautiful designs running a custom version of Android software. Those who dismissed Xiaomi as a mere copycat missed a key fact: that it was an entirely new and different type of smartphone company, unlike any before it.

For starters, Xiaomi puts out new phones monthly, a pace unprecedented for a high-end phone maker; Apple puts out a new version of its iPhone every 18 months to two years. Xiaomi also consults very closely with a community of millions of its customers in highly active and enthusiastic online forums; they constitute its most influential product managers. The company also pioneered a business model whereby it essentially sold phones at cost and sought to profit from the content and applications sold to run on the phones. This model has proven challenging, but it makes perfect sense. From online music and videos to high-end designer clothing and even furniture, many old business models of selling single items are being converted into subscription models.

For new business models and new ways in which customers interact with companies, it's often useful to look to China, where companies such as Xiaomi, Alibaba, and WeChat foretoken the future. That society of more than a billion people has sprinted ahead of Europe and the United States in many types of business innovation in how people interact with companies and with each other. In China, we see new ways in which companies can make money, with rapid-fire product development and extensive conversations between consumers and businesses. Western companies are increasingly emulating approaches originating in firms in Beijing or Shanghai.

In China, for example, audience recommendations guide a multi-billion-dollar market for subscriptions to home-grown online video channels—whose content often is the product of individuals in their bedrooms. In the United States, this process commenced with popular YouTubers; more recently, the online streaming platform Twitch (now part of Amazon) has emulated the Chinese strategy.

How quickly the structure of the game has changed.

This chapter details those changes. The failure by less innovative legacy companies to recognize them hampers severely their ability to innovate and transform. Here we detail six of the most basic structural marketplace changes that legacy companies struggle with.

Change 1: Shift in Power from Seller to Buyer

For starters, there has been a marked shift in power from seller to buyer through a reduction in information asymmetry. In the past, buyers of everything from cars to insurance and professional services had no way to know what others have experienced with these products or to aggregate useful opinions and ratings. Now they can connect with other buyers from across the globe and gain important insights before making purchasing decisions.

The Internet, although it has not entirely removed the information asymmetry, has strengthened buyers' knowledge of the market and thus their bargaining power. A new group of ratings intermediaries has emerged, and social networks have made it far easier to form groups and seek counsel from others with the insights and knowledge we seek, anywhere on the globe, at any time; they range from business-oriented social networks such as LinkedIn and enterprise-software rating and review sites such as G2 Crowd to the travel-rating site TripAdvisor. Yes, it is possible to cheat via these intermediaries; and there are limits on the information's context (e.g., whether the person providing the review shares your taste). But the only options available before the Internet were the recommendations of paid expert intermediaries, such as travel agents and consultants.

Change 2: Diminished Influence of Brand

In a similar vein, the security of brand equity has fallen dramatically. Customers, now able to choose on the basis of relevance to their immediate needs, are switching brands more easily—and one-third of respondents to a customer survey reported that they now "love to try new things."[1] Today, companies are constantly competing not only to attract new customers but also to keep their existing customers content to remain theirs.

Without a doubt, customers are now familiar with many more brands than they once were and are willing to try them out. In part, that's because customers are able to learn about and validate new brands, in both the consumer and business realms, through the greater number and variety of means of communication now available to them: Instagram, blogs, Snapchat, WhatsApp, Facebook, YouTube, and many more ways to reach a mass audience.

Change 3: Intellectual Capital Is "Leakier" Than Ever

In the realm of ideas and technical know-how, intellectual capital is far leakier than it was in the past—witness the job-hopping of engineers in autonomous vehicles and driverless cars as they launch new startup after new startup, each one utilizing knowledge and intellectual capital acquired at previous jobs.

The reality is that innovation is moving so quickly that the courts are no longer a viable mechanism to enforce intellectual capital in a way that actually polices transgressions. By the time a ruling is handed down, the new company may be worth more money than the one from which its engineers and intellectual capital came.

This leaves development of new products—or of new business models—the only way by which other companies can keep up.

Change 4: Product Development Cycles Move Much Faster

Legacy companies may be at some disadvantage in this respect because the cycles of product development that their ivory tower design teams favor limit creativity, leave out significant customer and market inputs, and confine innovation. Though Frog Design and IDEO may still design great products, a team fresh out of design school and working from a garage can compete with them on a nearly even footing and can more nimbly test customer sentiment and product viability—and often succeed precisely because it hasn't got the constraints that legacy companies do. Startups regularly measure market appetite by constructing landing pages selling products that they have yet to build. This is a move that an Apple, a Ford, or a Nike has never been comfortable doing.

Change 5: Technology Shifts Are Opening Massive New Markets

Despite a sincere desire and even their best efforts, most legacy firms lack both diversity and global perspective, blinding them to changing realities. First, they miss the massive new markets that technology shifts are opening beyond the developed world—and these market shifts may return to haunt them. (As we mentioned earlier in this chapter, China's technology-adoption practices have been preceding the West's, and frequently have presaged future consumer tastes in the United States and Europe.) Second, because traditional hierarchies and command-and-control structures are ineffective for knowledge workers and their needs, these firms can be slow to adapt old modes of work, leading younger workers to resent them. Third, the legacy companies tend to fall prey to the "Not Invented Here" syndrome rather than allow partnerships or collaborations to breathe fresh thinking into them.

Change 6: How We Communicate Has Changed—Changing Everything

In the old days, business communication occurred via memos, and gossip was spread around the water cooler. Now, information travels faster than wildfire, and everyone is always communicating—in a multitude of ways.

The social network TikTok, after launching in China as the short-video application Douyin in 2016 and absorbing a somewhat older U.S. short-video application, Musical.ly, in 2018, by the end of 2019 had fulfilled an astonishing 1.5 billion video downloads around the world.[2,3] To call TikTok a social network would be to understate its functions. It is more like a hybrid of YouTube, SnapChat, and Instagram that gives creators tools with which to instantly personalize common memes, but even that description fails to do TikTok justice. The system runs A.I. algorithms that seem to suggest the perfect meme videos for everyone's personal taste. Owned by the Chinese firm ByteDance, TikTok has grown so quickly that it has caught the eyes both of major corporate sponsors and of Western intelligence agencies, which fear an instrument of a foreign power that can gather so much intelligence and so easily influence such a large population of teenagers and young people.

TikTok joins Facebook, Snapchat, Instagram, Skype, WhatsApp, and Facetime as yet another communication app on our smartphones; but applications that begin with one function easily evolve to perform another. Gmail, for instance, integrates tightly with Google Hangouts, the company's free video-conferencing system; and, at work, Zoom has (especially during the COVID-19 crisis) become the most popular video-conferencing application to replace dreary landline conference calls. (The largely unaddressed problems in Zoom's privacy policy and misleading claim of end-to-end encryption, though, make other "large group chat" applications, such as Houseparty, Jitsi, and the particularly secure Signal, attractive alternatives.)

TikTok too illustrates the acceleration and diversification of communication. In parallel with the effects of other technologies' transfers from analog to digital, communications' digitization has predisposed it to control by software. As a result, the cost and other barriers to launching a full-blown communications network have fallen, and a small team of software engineers operating anywhere on Earth could launch the next disruptive communications application.

With the rise of the Internet, we leapt from phone calls, paper mail, and faxes to email, screen sharing, text messaging, and real-time video. We now stand on the cusp of a new form of reality sharing, one in which we can experience what others are seeing and doing, or share experiences, economically and all the time. Augmented-and virtual-reality applications have not yet hit the mainstream, but sales of the requisite gear are accelerating, and we are emerging from the trough of disappointment into the steep upward climb characteristic of the technology-adoption curves discussed earlier.

DIY, Cheap Communications Available to Everyone

This proliferation affects business innovation and growth too. Setting up the communications tools that a company needed used to necessitate an I.T. expert and a lot of money. Today, every knowledge worker already uses those tools as part of daily digital existence. Slack lets us not only chat but also share files and connect voice and video calls. Asana, Trello, and other project-management tools not only simplify communication within teams but also overlay email and Slack. For online storage of documents, we can use Google Drive, Box, Dropbox, Evernote, OneDrive, or any other of dozens of options.

Moreover, the cost of maintaining a communications infrastructure for a team is now a miniscule fraction of what it once was. In fact, it is entirely possible to set up everything necessary for creating, testing, and marketing products in less than an hour, online, for free. The smartphone is the biggest cost-reduction system ever introduced to humankind; each one now has, for free, devices and services that formerly cost tens of thousands of dollars in total, including the fax machine, scanner, media player, TV, video player, and camera, and even, for people comfortable with small devices, a laptop computer.

Unrestricted, Free Communications Means Loss of Control

The result of all this abundance is loss of control at all levels of authority, including the corporate level, as the tools of communication are now mastered and deployed by everyone with access to an Internet connection. That modern communication's ease and variety have made it mundane is what makes it critical to fostering innovation. As the great technology analyst and scholar Clay Shirky wrote in *Here Comes Everybody: The Power of Organizing without Organizations,* his seminal book on the impact of Internet technologies on organizations: "Communications tools don't get socially interesting until they get technologically boring."[4]

Open Access, Open Source, and Collective Product Development

An early instance of a collaboratively supported and created community entering and winning a legacy market was the Linux operating system. Created as a personal project by Finnish developer Linus Torvalds in 1991, Linux grew a community of users and developers through online collaboration and communication. Today, the upstart operating system is the dominant enterprise software: it powers the greatest number of core capabilities of servers that run the Internet, our communications networks, and our businesses. That community persists today and is embodied in the Linux Foundation, the steward of Linux and its ongoing development and one of the most powerful organizations in the software world even in 2020.

A Model of Collaborative Innovation

Management thinker Don Tapscott and business researcher Anthony D. Williams further fleshed out a model of collaborative innovation with their book *Wikinomics: How Mass Collaboration Changes Everything.*[5] The book was inspired by Wikipedia, the free user-generated online encyclopedia that supplanted the venerated *Encyclopedia Britannica* and came to be one of the most influential sources of online information in history. Edited as a collaborative effort by volunteers, Wikipedia serves as a fluid and sometimes controversial online test market for ideas and interpretations of history and facts. Based on his studies of Wikipedia, Tapscott lays out a theory of innovation whereby companies and organizations tap the collective intelligence of markets by facilitating and observing the results of mass collaboration on a global scale.

These same communications tools also give power to artists, musicians, and small businesses. Kevin Kelly, a co-founder of *Wired* magazine and a well-regarded technology thinker, laid the premise for this future business model built on community in 2008 with his brief article "1,000 True Fans."[6] The article's premise was that musicians, artists, and others could build an existence doing what they loved by identifying a small number of true fans and nurturing that community. Kelly himself proved his maxim with a stream of books, paid newsletters, and other offerings to his newsletter subscribers. Kelly's prescience took on further importance in the Internet age with the rise of crowdfunding sites such as Kickstarter, Indiegogo, and Patreon.

Legacy Communication Channels Are Withering

At the same time, legacy means of communication for marketing are diminishing in efficacy. Broadcast television, radio, and print are receiving decreasing shares of consumer attention. Even within each medium, the number of potential outlets is multiplying. Delivery of television and of short-form video news and content services has exploded, and podcasts are blurring into radio, further eroding that entire medium's market share. Although the drop in print readership has slowed in the past two years, the total promotional reach of newspapers and magazines is radically diminished. This works against incumbent brands that, because of advertising's high cost, formerly dominated these media. Broadcast television remains incredibly expensive, but advertisers are wary that major television networks may no longer deliver the same punch they once did.

How to reach customers has also become far less subject to legacy-company domination. Mass-media advertising and one-way messaging are losing efficacy; smart, focused digital advertising can cut through the noise. This digital scalpel is also accessible to anyone rather than just to the largest brands. In addition, as we have seen with SoulCycle, Toblerone, and many others, consumer and customer sentiment is just as easily influenced by social media, which can alter rapidly to render even the most thoughtful and resonant marketing useless and sully even the most respected brands.

Changes in Style, Substance, Mechanism, and Volume of Communications

This epochal shift in communication has come about through expansion in volume, style, and substance. We communicate now over many more platforms, including phone applications able to deliver text, voice, or video: a growing list that began with Skype, Messenger, WhatsApp, Facetime, and Slack. Even within companies, different teams use different systems.

How and how much we communicate has changed, increasing in traffic volume and transparency and shifting to a wider variety of media. This is true within companies too: employees communicate with each other all the time among locations, groups, divisions. Companies that fail to recognize it and continue to assume information asymmetry risk rebellion and ridicule. New tools, such as Facebook Groups and the anonymous professional network Blind, allow employees to organize and converse out of their employers' sight.

Collectively held mindsets driven by communication can either foster tremendous creativity or quickly destroy a company (or industry) culture. We are seeing the emergence of a new type of collective action and mindset, as the Google walkouts and the efforts to organize Uber and Lyft drivers exemplify. Even if this never emerges as truly organized labor, the era in which management had a strong information asymmetry is over, and it must behave accordingly or risk alienating its workforce and torching its reputation.

Vox Populi Gets Louder, Stronger

This new facility and fecundity of communications presents businesses with the double-edged sword of exponential risks and spectacular opportunities for rapid, targeted growth. The fitness-cycling chain SoulCycle was one of the massive business success stories of the 2010s, until it ran into a boycott buzzsaw arising from political dissent.

In August 2019, news outlets reported that a major SoulCycle investor, billionaire investor Stephen Ross, was planning to hold fundraisers for U.S. President Donald J. Trump. SoulCycle's primary clientele is urban upper-middle class women—a markedly anti-Trump demographic. When popular cooking celebrity Chrissy Teigen began tweeting in protest and calling for a boycott of the brand on Twitter, her missives gained hundreds of thousands of retweets.[7] Protest crowds formed outside SoulCycle studios and studios of another brand in which Ross had invested, the high-end gym company Equinox. The fallout for SoulCycle was brutal and swift. Class attendance plummeted. Even across the pond, at SoulCycle's studio in SoHo, London, attendance fell. The brand went from cool to cruel overnight, and the founding CEO of SoulCycle was forced to resign. Once targeted for an I.P.O., SoulCycle now faces an uncertain future.

In the span of a month, protests, rapidly spreading through social media, fueled a popular revolt that undermined a decade of work building a powerful brand. This is both a cautionary and a hopeful tale. With this explosion of media comes major decentralization of how a business talks with employees and customers, and of how members of both groups talk with each other. The same technology innovations that entertain us also empower customers and employees to organize, band together, and influence corporate and government behavior as never before. Uber legendarily used a plea for help in its phone app to drive a flood of emails and comments to the City Council of Washington, DC, when the city threatened to ban the ride-hailing app, and the Council quickly yielded.

At Facebook, ironically, employees used a rival network called Blind to vent grievances against their management as public debate raged over the company's advertising and privacy practices. Blind creates micro-networks that allow validated past and present employees to participate in a fully anonymized environment. Naturally, Facebook itself is not allowed representation on Blind (and attempts by HR teams to infiltrate the application were rapidly repelled by the participants). Google's engineers have organized walkouts using ad hoc communications tools to protest the search giant's work with the U.S. military and intelligence communities. In Europe, online outrage about a price hike and size diminution in the triangle thickness of the famed Toblerone chocolate bar led maker Mondelez International to revert to the bar's previous dimensions.

Such cases illustrate the drawbacks that democratization of communication can represent for businesses wishing to keep a lid on dissension, internal or external. But the commercial benefits too of communications' decentralization and proliferation are manifest. We have already seen how Dollar Shave Club tapped into the virality of YouTube to build a billion-dollar business. Savvy entrepreneurs are tapping into digital tools to craft focused go-to-market strategies that stimulate demand and lower the costs of potential failure.

From Zero to $600 Million in Five Short Years

In 2013, two childhood friends, Peter Rahal and Jared Smith, started making protein bars in their kitchen near Chicago, Illinois. They created recipes for plant-based, minimally processed bars that they thought would appeal to the growing crowd of adherents to minimalist eating principles. Those principles—few ingredients, all understandable in plain language—were popularized by author Michael Pollan and new diets such as Paleo and Whole30. Rahal and Smith initially handed out samples of their RXBAR products to CrossFit practitioners. Rather than spend money on fancy packaging design, Rahal and Smith designed their packaging in PowerPoint. It was simple and readable.

The entrepreneurs' timing and approach were impeccable. But what allowed RXBAR to grow quickly and effectively was a digital-first strategy that focused on online ads and other marketing to its target markets. Rahal and Smith sold their product using Google and Facebook ads, testing and learning and fine-tuning to get the most from every dollar they spent, later expanding to more than two dozen digital channels and aggressively positioning their product on Amazon.com and other online marketplaces.

Only after all of this did RXBAR create a brick-and-mortar strategy to gain broad access to supermarkets and other physical locations. By then, the company's brand was well established and it had a base of loyal customers, most of whom paid a monthly fee to have a box of bars delivered to their home or office. With that wind at their backs, Rahal and Smith could enter new establishments relatively confident that their tasty bars would sell. They also knew they could easily test and experiment with new products in an economical and iterative manner, running circles around legacy food companies that take years to perfect and test recipes.

By turning the traditional strategy for entering the specialty food market on its head, Rahal and Smith were able to grow faster and far more cheaply. They did not have to pay for trucks, representatives, distributors, or any of the usual accoutrements of traditional businesses marketing energy bars and other consumer packaged goods.

This new way of using digital communications channels and distribution strategies has become a path to success for a growing number of hot brands. A cooking-appliance sensation, InstaPots, followed a similar "Amazon-first" and digital-only path. Allbirds shoes sold online only before eventually opening a handful of small stores.

Really, this was all about communicating and using modern communication tools as advantages in cutting through the noise, promoting a brand, testing a product, or building a community. In interviews, Rahal and Smith have frequently cited "building a community" as a key part of their successful journey. This is a phrase that would probably not have entered the lexicon of a CEO even two decades earlier. Indeed, the idea of using cheap technology to build a community that supports and buys a product can trace its ascent to the rise of the Internet.

6

What Has Not Changed

CHAPTER SUMMARY: This chapter covers how legacy companies may develop exponential technology or other innovations but be unable to effectively and sustainably make products of them. We review the causes of the failure of Google Wallet (later Google Pay Send) and other innovations—including creating the wrong incentives for partners, failing to upgrade products quickly enough, and failing to retain innovation leaders who want to move faster and create more.

What Went Wrong with Google Wallet

In 2011, to great fanfare, Google announced Google Wallet, a mobile payment app and ecosystem that the search giant claimed would finally push American and European customers to ditch plastic and use their phones to pay for everything. Wallet cost hundreds of millions of dollars to create and required a massive business development effort that included partnerships with credit card processor and financial-services behemoth Mastercard, big bank Citi, wireless carrier Sprint, and others. In introducing Wallet, the head of the effort, Google Payments' V.P., Osama Bedier, called it "one of the biggest investments" Google had ever made. "This is just the start of what has already been a great adventure towards the future of mobile shopping. We're incredibly excited and hope you are, too," wrote Google Wallet founding engineers Jonathan Wall and Rob von Behren in the introductory blog post.[1]

Reviewers and the tech press lauded Google Wallet. The mood was celebratory. And yet, two years later, only a small number of users had downloaded Google Wallet and were using it on their Android devices. Negative press was accumulating, and consumers yawned at several efforts to reintroduce Wallet.

Right Product, Right Vision, Wrong Approach

Clearly the concept of mobile payments had not been misplaced. Since launching Apple Pay in 2014, Google rival Apple has steadily gained ground in mobile payments; it is now used by tens of millions of people each day in the United States and Europe. In Europe, contactless payments too have taken off (but nothing compared to China, where cash is going out of vogue). Large retailers Starbucks and Walmart have successfully marketed their branded mobile-payment applications; and Starbucks trails only Apple in adoption, even though its app is useful only for purchasing coffee or food at its stores. Google's own Google Pay has gained a good amount of market share since the failure of Wallet but still trails Apple and Starbucks by a large margin as of this writing.[2]

Perhaps most damning of all, Bedier left Google and went on to launch Poynt, a maker of new point-of-sale software and hardware that embraces contactless payments. Poynt has raised nearly $300 million and is almost certain to have a successful exit. Among its funders is, ironically, Google Ventures, the venture-capital arm of Google.

Google was the first big mover. It had clearly seen the future and had built a product that worked pretty well. So what had it gotten so wrong?

Inflexibility in Its Business Model

Unlike Apple, Google had insisted that the wireless carriers, banks, and payment-processing entities share purchase data with Google. This was consistent with the premise of Google's entire business model: offering free services and collecting granular user data. But Google has always pursued this transaction via a direct relationship with the customer. In this case, Google was taking information that is the lifeblood of many of its partners. Predictably, this spooked the very partners and would-be partners vital to Google's access to it.

It's true that there were other problems. Google Wallet landed when only two-thirds of the developed world's population had begun using smartphones. Additionally, Wallet depended on point-of-sale terminals capable of contactless communication, which did not become widespread in the United States until after 2015. In both contexts, Apple's timing was better. But Google certainly had the financial wherewithal to wait for those trends to catch up with its product. The fatal problem was the flaw in its business model that entailed taking someone else's lunch: customer data. In the grand scheme of things, that may seem like a small miss. In modern business, though, business-model failures are the worst kind, because they so often become evident after massive investments have been made in engineering, design, and marketing.

Surprisingly, failure is par for the course for Google: the company has racked up a long array of technology failures despite its reputation as one of the most innovative companies in history. Apple, which launches far fewer products, has far fewer massive failures and has shown an ability to expand into new markets far more smoothly than Google. This is in part because Apple has proven its flexibility in its business arrangements and its willingness to adapt and innovate in its business models in order to meet situational requirements.

Failure to Launch, Adapt, Change, and Take Risks

The reality is that most of the great technology successes we read about are based on ideas that were borrowed or stolen from other companies or labs. Almost every single innovation attributed to Apple emerged from something that the Cupertino behemoth either acquired or copied. And examples abound of legacy companies' creating amazing technology on which others later capitalize: Xerox PARC and the mouse, Cisco video conferencing and Zoom, the spreadsheet (Lotus 1-2-3) and Microsoft Excel, and so forth.

This is unsurprising in light of the penalties, overt or tacit, that risk-taking generally attracts. Even though tech companies trumpet failure as a badge of determination, none reward failed project leaders with promotions or raises for their manifest ambition. Like Google Wallet's project lead, who left the company to launch a startup, many of the highest-paid employees tend to be in roles that penalize risk and most handsomely reward constancy. This is because Wall Street, which drives the strategy of so many legacy companies, generally has very low tolerance for failure, making it much harder for public companies to take big risks. The demand for constancy and predictability results in tight, top-down hierarchies, causing risk-averse companies to become painfully slow in decision-making and product development. With such internal inertia, all too often, even when the disruption is obvious—as in the disruption of phone companies by Skype—they cannot contrive a response that is effective or even meaningful.

The variable critical to creating innovative ideas in these companies is the time, thinking space, and other resources afforded to employees. Some companies, such as Amazon, have systematized this process: it offers employees with ideas in approved product areas a startup grant and other incentives to encourage them to start that company. The implicit promise, moreover, is that, should their venture fail, Amazon will welcome them back into the fold.

For its part, Amazon has elevated failure to a high art. It is one of the few very large companies that not only accepts failure but expects it in its most ambitious experimental new products and services. Google famously has encouraged internal startups in a similar fashion, but without the same results: only one major product success, Gmail, has emerged from internal startups. (Some might count Google G Suite corporate applications, but those lag far behind Microsoft's Office365 online suite of tools everywhere except in Silicon Valley.)

Amazon's methods probably don't, though, herald a future in which innovative ideas will receive their due and nurture in large companies. Even Google has been cutting back on the innovation time it allows to engineers; and Apple, long the model of corporate innovation, is among the most top-down companies in terms of product innovation and management.

Cisco's Failure and the Rise of Zoom

Eric Yuan had a problem. As the vice president in charge of Cisco's collaboration and video-conferencing unit, he had lots of ideas on how to make his products better and more beloved by users. But he got the company's practical support for hardly any of them—despite leading the unit.

The year was 2011, and Cisco was the dominant player in the field. It competed with Polycom for high-end videoconferencing software and equipment, and with GoToMeeting for lower-end corporate videoconferencing contracts; but Cisco was the overall market leader. Cisco's general bet on videoconferencing's being a growth industry had paid off. The unit had posted sales and profit growth that outstripped that of the legacy networking equipment businesses.

But no one loved Cisco's collaboration and meeting products. They were unreliable, often requiring that users install them multiple times on the same machine for no apparent reason. Though the innovative products like virtual-reality conferencing were well received, Cisco left the lower end of its market starved for innovation and improvements, and small fit-and-finish details were left by the wayside. For example, a one-touch dial-in option would have saved people who were calling into Webex the enormous hassle of flipping back and forth between invitation text and the application merely in order to enter the meeting's code (which was always a seven-digit number, just long enough to be hard for humans to remember). And then there was the problem of bandwidth: Webex hogged it and delivered poor quality except when connectivity was perfect.

All these problems were noted and cataloged by Yuan, a super-smart and motivated Chinese engineer who came to Cisco with the Webex acquisition in 2007. Yuan initially set out to fix them inside Cisco. As he said in a 2017 interview, "I was paid very well as a VP at Cisco. But Webex was my baby. In 2010 and 2011, I did not see happy customers. I was very embarrassed that I spent so much time on the technology. Why are the customers not happy?"[3]

The Innovator Leaves, Starts His Own Thing, and Zooms Away

Yuan finally had had enough and left Cisco, taking with him roughly 40 of the top engineers from Webex. His new goal was to make a universal tool for videoconferencing that users loved. It would work as well in a coffee shop as on a corporate campus. It would gracefully handle fluctuations in bandwidth. And it would be incredibly easy to use. Yuan named it Zoom. He decided to try a bottom-up freemium strategy that allowed anyone to set up an account for free 40-minute meetings of a limited number of participants. Zoom would sell upgrades for longer meetings, storage of online recordings, and management tools, as well as dedicated videoconferencing hardware for higher-fidelity meetings. Eight years after launching, Zoom went public and quickly achieved a market capitalization in excess of $20 billion. Yuan's retooled videoconferencing product has won rave reviews. And, in the true mark of market dominance, it has become a verb in the vernacular of its users. Although Cisco has publicly denied it, many analysts believe that Zoom has stolen considerable market share from Cisco.

The tale of Zoom illustrates not only that legacy companies fail in launches of new products because they tend to view the world through the lens of existing business models but also that they struggle mightily to fix basic, obvious problems in their existing dominant products. Implementing such reforms would seem an obvious opportunity. But, as anyone who has spent time pitching for placement on a product roadmap can attest, the bigger the company and the more engineers depending on the roadmap, the harder it is to make any real headway in a timely fashion.

7

The Eight Deadly Sins That Disable Change Efforts

CHAPTER SUMMARY: In this chapter, we cover eight common attitudes, approaches, and errors that can negate innovation efforts, using a wide range of real-world examples of how these sins can harm a business and even drive it into insolvency.

In their excellent book *Lead and Disrupt,*[1] Stanford University's Charles O'Reilly and Harvard's Mike Tushman compellingly present a means for companies to avoid the Innovator's Dilemma; they also analyze how a handful of companies, including Amazon and IBM, have managed to successfully pivot to new opportunities without concurrently sacrificing their old businesses. In the case of Amazon, for example, the company has disrupted itself with innovation not just once or twice but many times. Two of those innovations—Amazon Web Services (the cloud-computing business) and Amazon's advertising business—will probably be the most profitable parts of Jeff Bezos's empire. Amazon was able to do this without slowing down any of its retail operations, according to the authors, because it practices what the authors call *ambidextrous leadership*. This phrase describes a delicate balance between giving internal startups and innovation projects the room they need in order to breathe, the funding they need in order to grow, and the executive sponsorship they require in order to avoid being eaten or crippled by legacy business units.

We will talk more about their theories in the last section of this book. But what are equally instructive are their insights on what kills innovation in large legacy companies and prevents them from generating new lines of business. From our own observations over time, and our own experience working inside or advising large organizations, we have formed our own hypotheses on what makes large organizations so unable to embrace change and risk. There is some overlap between our observations and O'Reilly and Tushman's findings.

We call our observations the Eight Deadly Sins of Stasis. Those sins are:

1. Unwillingness to listen
2. Lack of patience
3. Lack of distance
4. Lack of resources
5. Wrong people and wrong role
6. Lack of accountability
7. Inappropriate culture
8. Lack of political support

We will quickly run through each of these sins and supply an example from the past of how it played out in a real-world instance. Individually, none of these sins will doom a company to oblivion in its efforts to innovate and change. Collectively, though, they are a strong indicator that a company's entire culture is stymying its efforts to maintain its relevance and survive. To put it bluntly, an organization that suffers from these sins probably has a larger cultural problem to overcome.

1. Unwillingness to Listen

Toyota employees meet regularly to suggest process improvements. This comes from a culture of listening wherein even top executives are willing to listen to employees far down the ranks. This can and ideally will extend beyond the confines of the company into customers, consultants, and partners. When a company has a listening culture, the very act of listening opens it to change. Part of the reason that Amazon has been able to launch so many new business lines so quickly is that it is constantly listening to its marketplace by watching the data coursing through its commercial and technological veins. For its part, despite its failings, Google has always been a company that listens well to employees for new ideas. This is evidenced in the "20 percent time" it afforded to engineers to pursue passion projects. Other historically innovative companies too have had the characteristic of good listeners.

Firms that have failed to listen have often failed to adapt. A case in point is the British retailer HMV. Once a paragon of cool in Britain and the power broker in the hot worlds of pop music, films, and video games, HMV experienced a spectacular fall from grace when all three of its major business lines were savaged by online competition. In a telling article explaining the demise of HMV, advertising executive Philip Beeching recounts a 2002 meeting with HMV's management team where he detailed the three greatest threats to the company: online retailers, downloadable music, and supermarkets' discounting. Beeching narrates what happened next:

> Suddenly I realised the MD had stopped the meeting and was visibly angry. "I have never heard such rubbish," he said, "I accept that supermarkets are a thorn in our side but not for the serious music, games, or film buyer, and as for the other two, I don't ever see them being a real threat, downloadable music is just a fad and people will always want the atmosphere and experience of a music store rather than online shopping."[2]

HMV's management team was unwilling to listen. The company ignored the online perils until too late and failed to ever build a viable online presence or to explore alternative business models more suited to an age of decreasing purchases of discs of music or films. Weighted down by poor management, HMV went bankrupt twice, in 2013 and in 2018, after shuttering most of its stores.

Had it but listened.

2. Lack of Patience

Innovation takes time to build and gestate—despite being all about moving fast. That is the paradox and a crucial balance. A significant percentage of startups pivot to a new business model or product during their early years. Some do so more than once. Many startups labor for three years or more before even achieving product-market fit, that golden connection showing that you have something customers want, need, and will pay for. Though interminable patience is equally damaging (see the section on lack of accountability), a dearth of patience spells certain doom for innovation and internal efforts to chart new courses.

In March 2016, the Mozilla Connected Devices team launched a new project called SensorWeb, a crowdsourced web of PM2.5 air quality sensors. The project was started by a Mozilla engineer in Taipei, Taiwan, who wanted an easy way for her grandmother to access immediate air quality information on a smartphone or a computer. As part of the browser company and nonprofit's exploration of Internet-of-Things devices, Project SensorWeb was one of several efforts to develop new business models. Mozilla produced dozens of PM2.5 sensor kits and distributed them for free, and the project produced spectacular maps of air quality and garnered a loyal following. But, less than a year after launch, Mozilla abruptly shut the project down.

As global warming continues to cause massive fires around the world, air quality has become a bigger and more pressing concern. In the United States, a company called PurpleAir launched a similar effort to sell and link high-quality PM2.5 sensors. During the California wildfires of 2018 and 2019, PurpleAir became the go-to source for local air-quality information, with the best coverage in California by far. Is there a business opportunity there? As we look at the successful exits of Weather.com and the acquisition of the Weather Underground by IBM, it appears that perhaps Project SensorWeb was unplugged too soon.

3. Lack of Distance

In his book *The Innovator's Dilemma,* Clayton Christensen advocates forming external businesses to compete with parent companies. Only by separating completely, he argues, can disruptive innovation thrive and grow. O'Reilly and Tushman, in contrast, hold that companies should create some distance but that growing new business lines internally is viable if they get a dedicated budget and executive sponsorship.[3] In our view, either option is viable, but the most important commonality is that new business lines be allowed the space and distance required to explore their new opportunities with fresh eyes.

Distance includes not only physical distance—separate offices—but also distance from many of the existing processes of the legacy companies. For example, part of what allows startups to move so quickly is that they are not burdened by rigorous compliance processes and I.T. requirements. Moreover, they don't need fancy videoconferencing gear or fancy office furniture. What they need are speed, agility, and the right to distance themselves from internal status quos in order to move faster. They need the autonomy that distance provides.

O'Reilly and Tushman cite an example in which a Hewlett-Packard unit cannibalized funding for an innovative new type of printing system's R&D efforts in order to refocus on developing legacy product lines. Another classic example of lack of distance killing a product's chances was the Nike FuelBand. An early wearable device that competed with Fitbit and other fitness trackers, the FuelBand won over early converts with its clean design and its nifty social functions encouraging competition between users. But the FuelBand suffered from too much internal control; the engineering team making the band knew that it would need to be better integrated with smartphones and had to quickly iterate features. Nike's internal product-development cadence and more stately pace could not handle this, and, over time, features on the product lagged far behind those of other fitness trackers. Yes, LeBron James wore one, but users simply wanted one that worked well with both iPhone and Android. In 2014, Nike killed the FuelBand after a two-year run.[4] Many from the team that had worked on it moved over to Apple, joining the Apple Watch team, a product that is quickly becoming a sleeper hit for Apple CEO Tim Cook.

4. Lack of Resources

Though it is important that corporate innovation be nimble and not too resource dependent, neither should it starve. Resources take on many forms: office space, budgets, personnel, R&D lab capacity, legal resources, and more. Too many resources can lead to more stasis and product-development paralysis. A resource shortage, though, is a more common malady, often killing innovation efforts before birth. Too few resources—in the form of either a hard "No" or steady starvation—also signal to intrapreneurs that their efforts are not prioritized and that they are wasting their time. As we saw Zoom did to Eric Yuan, a company can starve innovators of resources through simple neglect.

Some companies take innovative approaches to assigning necessary resources. 3M has long had a 15 percent policy (call it the original Google 20 percent) to allow employees to focus on projects. Once a year, 3M employees from across the company create posters showing off their projects. They all stand in an auditorium, and thousands of 3M employees parade by, reading the posters and offering feedback and suggestions. If they are so inspired, employees are empowered to join a project as a collaborator. By letting employees vote with their feet, 3M creates a viable marketplace for internal ideas and a neat way to assign resources to the most persuasive. This approach has granted critical human capital to numerous products that later made it to market—from painter's tape to reflective optical films and clear bandages.[5]

5. Wrong People and Wrong Role

All too often, internal innovation teams are set up with leaders who are masters of getting things done in the broad company organization. Likewise, engineers or designers are picked from the most successful teams in the bigger company. But what makes someone successful in a large company usually does not carry over to applied innovation and internal startups.

Success in the larger entity means following the process and sticking to the rules—bending them only a little, if at all. In applying innovation and moving quickly, such commitments become obstacles. You need executives, engineers, and designers who, though they may have been successful in these other contexts, as often as not have struggled because they had a different vision or wanted to try new ways of doing things. This is why, in building his team for *The Incredibles 2* at Pixar, director Brad Bird hired a cadre of restless company "black sheep" to reimagine the delivery of video special effects and make a movie faster than anyone had ever envisaged.

As Bird related in an interview with consultancy McKinsey & Co.:

> I said, "Give us the black sheep. I want artists who are frustrated. I want the ones who have another way of doing things that nobody's listening to. Give us all the guys who are probably headed out the door." A lot of them were malcontents because they saw different ways of doing things, but there was little opportunity to try them, since the established way was working very, very well. We gave the black sheep a chance to prove their theories, and we changed the way a number of things are done here. For less money per minute than was spent

on the previous film, *Finding Nemo,* we did a movie that had three times the number of sets and had everything that was hard to do. All this because the heads of Pixar gave us leave to try crazy ideas.[6]

6. Lack of Accountability

Innovation is sexy and fun. But too many legacy companies view innovation goals as pet projects rather than as serious initiatives. Creating an attitude and environment of ". . . and if it works out, great!" is a terrible way to affirm innovation's importance. This kind of environment, though common, transpires only if innovation efforts face no real accountability or regular hard questioning. You can see, of course, that many of the failed innovation structures we discussed—such as corporate outposts in Silicon Valley and internal corporate innovation teams—all too often can fall into this trap of lack of accountability. Worse still, this environment can attract precisely the wrong sorts of executive sponsors to innovation projects: sponsors who lack real commitment and see innovation efforts as yet another way to burnish their resumes.

Sometimes, lack of accountability can have dire consequences. After decades of superlative results, Cisco Systems CEO John Chambers adopted a new management structure that created a series of councils and new management boards with the goal of pushing decision-making power down to a group of 500 or so executives and leaders. The idea was to stimulate communications across Cisco and raise the overall metabolism of the flagging networking giant, accelerating its progress.[7] As part of that effort, Chambers saddled executives with sitting on the boards of promising innovation efforts, but left vague the criteria for what constituted a promising effort. And the innovation assignment was just one of the numerous new committee and internal board and project assignments doled out to the leaders.

The so-called matrix management system quickly soured many of Cisco's leaders, who felt bogged down in a high volume of meetings and discussions that, perversely, slowed decision-making. As you can imagine, for executives suddenly stuck on dozens of committees, an innovation project with no real accountability lacked priority. Without genuine executive interest, internal innovation efforts failed to gain significant traction or generate new products. Two years later, after hundreds of leadership departures from Cisco, Chambers admitted he had made a mistake with his management structure. Cisco's stalled innovation efforts, which failed to produce internal innovation on par with the company's aggressive acquisition strategy, were a predictable casualty. To date, the company continues to struggle with incorporating internal innovation efforts into product development.

7. Inappropriate Culture

Poisonous internal politics, inconsistently applied or unclear rules, and paralysis due to fear will block any business's progress.

Though many studies have demonstrated a direct correlation between a healthy, productive culture and a company's ability to transform, most businesses still spend little time thinking about, let alone acting to improve, their internal culture—despite the contribution that a negative culture will make to reducing employee engagement, stifling creativity, and increasing employee turnover.

Xerox invented most of the technologies that we use in personal computing today, but it now plays little role in computing. Kodak invented the digital camera yet filed for bankruptcy in 2012. Nokia was a pioneer of the smartphone and still lost its leadership position to Apple's iPhone. These companies didn't use their positions of strength to transform, and so missed their crucial market opportunities. Kodak, in particular, which was afraid to compete with its own traditional film business and therefore of innovating, focused only on the next quarter when it should have been thinking about the possible long-term gains.

Two CEOs who have understood the importance of culture in transforming iconic businesses are Lou Gerstner at IBM and Satya Nadella at Microsoft.

Gerstner joined IBM in 1993 and developed a strategy to use processes and culture to regain advantage. Moving from proprietary standards to open standards, for example, was important to IBM's new strategy in light of dramatic adoption of Internet and web technologies, and IBM had to learn to open up and even give away base technologies, creating value by solving customers' problems using systems built on its business processes.

Underneath all the sophisticated processes, Gerstner concluded, there is always the company's sense of values and identity.

> It took me to age fifty-five to figure that out. I always viewed culture as one of those things you talked about, like marketing and advertising. It was one of the tools that a manager had at his or her disposal when you think about an enterprise. The thing I have learned at IBM is that culture is everything.[8]

In the six years following Microsoft's hiring of Satya Nadella as CEO in 2014, its share price tripled. Nadella has been lauded for successfully repositioning the business from a "devices and services" company to a "mobile and cloud" company. But Nadella always states that Microsoft's reinvention would have been impossible without changing the culture among his 130,000 employees.

In an interview in *McKinsey Quarterly,* Nadella states:

> there's no such thing as a perpetual-motion machine. At some point, the concept or the idea that made you successful is going to run out of gas. So you need new capability to go after new

concepts. The only thing that's going to enable you to keep building new capabilities and trying out new concepts long before they are conventional wisdom is culture.[9]

Nadella's emphasis on developing a learning company based on the growth mindset, one that is constantly seeking to develop and improve, has delivered spectacular results.

It's worth noting that bad behaviors can infect the business and do tremendous damage.

A fantastic example of a team culture that understands this and looks to eradicate bad behavior is the New Zealand rugby union team, known as the All Blacks. The most successful rugby team of all time, with a win rate of 80 percent, it refuses to tolerate bad behavior that threatens the balance of the team or *whanau,* the Maori word for extended family. There is no room for prima donnas, and everyone must work together toward the same goal.

8. Lack of Political Support

As we noted earlier in this chapter, enabling innovation requires resources, patience, distance, and a willingness to lead. All of these are dependent on innovation efforts receiving enough political support to fend off other parts of the organization that would rather these fledgling efforts died.

Corporate budgets are political allocations as hotly contested as government budgets are. For the CEO and her team, a budget is a bet on the future with clear winners and losers every year. For any general manager with discretion as to how to spend his unit's budget, his choice of which team gets how much is a statement of his priorities and allegiances.

It's almost always politically expedient to starve innovation efforts in order to feed the hungry mouths you already have that are proven revenue generators. Innovation efforts without robust support by an executive sponsor are far more likely to be cherry-picked and left to starve. The Cisco example demonstrates this indirectly; because so many executives were busy trying to sponsor and mentor so many different innovation efforts, all of them suffered a collective lack of political support. It was a tragedy of the innovation commons.

A Struggle for Balance

The Eight Deadly Sins have many overlapping facets, and they hint at a key reality for managing innovation efforts effectively within organizations: a constant struggle for balance. Too much is as bad as too little. Too far is as bad as too close. Recalibrating all these settings on a constant basis to ensure that an organization maintain the right balance poses a significant management challenge.

PART III

Ways to Build Innovative, Exponentially Developing Companies

Over the past two decades, we have participated in dozens of innovation exercises with numerous companies. We have guided legacy energy giants in creating market opportunities by taking risks on innovations and better business models. We have helped retail chains and supermarkets defend themselves against Amazon and other online-only vendors. We have helped financial-services institutions defend themselves and then partner with financial-technology companies and have helped a national government to rethink the resource allocation, recruitment strategy, and future requirements of its army. Unlike most innovation experts, we have also served as senior executives overseeing major innovation efforts. At Accenture, Ismail served as a senior executive driving change for global clients; at IBM, he lived through one of the most difficult innovation periods in recent history as Big Blue pivoted for a third time. Vivek has helped build two successful software companies, one of which went public with $120 million in revenue in a short five years. As an academic, he has been conducting masterclasses and workshops on exponential innovation for some of the largest companies in the world.

We have also read as much of the relevant research as we could. In doing so, we realized that research on innovation is of wildly varying quality. We believe that, between our real-world experience and our (over) exposure to academic thinking and models on the topic, we have come to understand what works and what doesn't. This is why we wrote the book. And in this section, we will share with you what we have learned.

8

"Don't Buy This Jacket": Subverting Retail Expectations

CHAPTER SUMMARY: This brief chapter covers business-model innovation as practiced by a highly regarded clothing manufacturer and retailer and the ways in which turning traditional business models on their head (and even doing things that would seem to cannibalize the existing business) can yield strong positive outcomes.

It may have been the first time that an upscale global retail brand vehemently and publicly urged its customers not to purchase its products on the biggest shopping day of the year (Figure 8.1).

But that's precisely what Patagonia did on Black Friday in November 2011, with a splashy ad campaign bearing a subversive message to shoppers: "Don't Buy This Jacket."[1] The ad spot, which ran in *The New York Times*, was the Southern California company's cheeky way to draw attention to Patagonia's newly launched Common Threads environmental initiative.

Figure 8.1. Patagonia's Counter intuitive Marketing of Recycled Clothing. An iconic advertisement by Patagonia, Inc. promoting their new used marketplace
Source: Image Credit: Patagonia, Inc.

The ad went on to detail the environmental impact of each one of the R2 jackets pictured in the ad: 135 liters of water (enough to meet the daily needs of 45 people) used in manufacture, and nearly 20 pounds of carbon dioxide (nearly 24 times the weight of the jacket) released in transporting it. The copy on the ad went further with an anti-consumption message. "Because Patagonia wants to be in business for a good long time—and leave a world inhabitable for our kids—we want to do the opposite of every other business today. We ask you to buy less and to reflect before you spend a dime on this jacket or anything else."

The goal of Common Threads was to encourage people to consider buying used clothing in order to maximize the environmental awareness of apparel making. Earlier in 2011, Patagonia had teamed up with eBay to launch a branded store for reselling gently worn Patagonia clothes and gear on eBay. To encourage adoption, Patagonia elected not to make any money on the transaction; eBay users were selling just as they would normally. All that was required for them to list or shop on the microsite inside eBay was that they sign the Common Threads Pledge, in which they pledged to buy and sell used Patagonia clothing to each other whenever possible rather than buy a new item.

A decade later, that counter intuitive thinking has created a growing new revenue stream for Patagonia, burnishing its environmental reputation by pursuing a fast-growing consumer trend: re-use and resale of high-end clothing. Patagonia has an entire section on its website dedicated to the resale of used clothing that meet high standards (in some cases, even reconditioned by the company).

And when you walk into the Patagonia store on Pearl Street, a shopping stretch in Boulder, Colorado, popular among the well-to-do, you will find the first permanent location of the descendant of the original Common Threads initiative, Patagonia's Worn Wear program. The store within a store is a resale boutique, likely to be the first of many in Patagonia's U.S. stores. The Boulder store incorporated its permanent Worn Wear boutique after the brand had tested the concept in dozens of pop-up shops around the country. The slogan of the Worn Wear program is clever: "These clothes are made from other clothes."

Patagonia has been living up to its environmental values (and using them as marketing tools) for many years. It first began recycling clothes in 2005. It also takes back and melts down polyester products to re-use the materials in new products. But recycling, the company concluded, was not as effective in environmental conservation as simply encouraging greater and lengthier use of Patagonia clothes.

At its Boulder Worn Wear shop, Patagonia runs a consignment store where shoppers can trade in, repair, and shop for used items. Ironically, this may actually encourage more shoppers to buy the expensive Patagonia items, because they calculate that it will be easier (and less of a hassle) to return them to Patagonia for store credit. Patagonia repairs more than a hundred thousand articles of clothing each year, most worth greater than $50 on the resale market. Though Patagonia does not disclose revenues, this new revenue stream is likely to bring the brand millions of dollars in "found money" annually—and retail analysts believe that the Worn Wear program has only boosted sales of new Patagonia clothing.[2]

A (Business) World Turned Upside Down—And That's a Good Thing

As Patagonia exemplifies in telling shoppers not to buy its product, the best ways of fostering innovation may not be obvious at first glance. More often than not, the very best innovation ideas come from an unexpected contributor, a branch office, or an afterthought. (As our journalist friends often say, the best quotes come the minute you shut off the recorder.) We chose the Patagonia example because it is so striking and yet so satisfying, in that it has nearly ideal outcomes though the tactics to get there are certainly not standard business-school fare. In the remaining chapters, we will investigate how to apply these ideas and make them work; but let's first look at why it is that these new business models are dominating innovation.

9

Platform Technologies and Marketplaces

CHAPTER SUMMARY: This chapter covers how the new digital-business models that have led to rapid growth and profits by the large technology companies arise from new technologies. Platform technologies tend to share certain dynamics, including network effects, efficient distribution, and asymmetric growth.

The transformation of "Don't Buy This Jacket" into a full-blown business line selling repurposed and restored wares has the potential to markedly increase the value that Patagonia obtains through every sale item. Unlocking this profit engine demonstrates the potential of two of the new business models that the exponentially advancing technologies have facilitated: marketplaces and platforms.

Marketplaces have existed since time immemorial as places where people gather for commerce. From Istanbul's Grand Bazaar to Oxford Street in London and the shopping malls that dot the suburbs of the United States, marketplaces are omnipresent. Virtual marketplaces, however, are both more accessible and more profitable than physical ones, because they are not constrained by physical real estate or brochure page count. Indeed, Amazon's entire conceit is to create an "endless shelf" that easily bears the weight of hundreds of millions of products, far more than any brick-and-mortar store could ever handle. The Internet and ubiquitous connectivity make establishment of a marketplace easy: eBay, Amazon, PayPal, and many others succeeded as a result of the ease of building them.

From Marketplaces to Platforms That Support Entire Ecosystems

In a variation on marketplaces, platform businesses have emerged as the most powerful forces in global business. Platforms allow others to build businesses on top of them. By creating a new source of value with innovative products and capabilities, platforms allow many others to benefit, increasing every vendor's profit. Most of the blockbuster technology successes of the late 1990s and early 2000s have been platform technologies. Salesforce, Facebook, Google, Microsoft, and Amazon are all classic examples. As of this writing, the five most valuable publicly traded companies in the world—Apple, Google, Microsoft, Amazon, and Facebook—are all platform companies, and collectively worth more than $3 trillion. The seventh-and eighth-most valuable are Chinese platform companies Alibaba and Tencent. The ninth-most valuable company, Visa, is a platform company as well.

Across public and private markets, KPMG calculated that, as of 2018, the world's top 242 platform companies had a collective market value exceeding $7 trillion, 187 of them being worth more than $1 billion each.[1] One of these, Amazon Web Services (a unit inside Amazon), would probably be among the top 15 most valuable companies in the world if it were an independent company, and Google's YouTube and Apple's App Store would probably be in the Fortune 100.

Transaction Platforms, Innovation Platforms, Combined Platforms

For the most part, platforms are online matchmakers or technology frameworks. The most common types are *transaction platforms,* which bring together buyers and sellers and provide tools for their efficient use by either side; examples are eBay and Airbnb.

Apple, for example, hosts an App Store where developers can sell software products (games, applications) and publishers can sell content (music, movies, books, magazines). Apple also provides the software frameworks necessary for third parties to build applications on the Apple platform.

Other transaction platforms include Amazon, Airbnb, Uber, and Baidu.

A second platform type, the *innovation platform,* provides a common technology framework for businesses to build upon, and benefits both the platform provider and those who build on it or use it. For example, Salesforce is an innovation platform in that it supports thousands of independent companies that develop and sell their own software products based on the Force.com framework.

The most powerful platform companies tend to be both transaction and innovation platforms: *combined platforms.* Facebook is one such: it is both a marketplace where people can buy casual games and ads, and a place where developers can create and sell games and monetize content, using Facebook's technology.

Platform businesses are found on every populated continent. The M-Pesa mobile-payments platform, in Africa, is believed to be the first broadly accepted platform for mobile payments, before WePay and Alipay in China.

Platforms can be built on software-controlled physical devices too. Tesla's cars; DJI's drones; and Apple's, Amazon's, and Google's voice assistants are all platforms comprising physical devices and software.

The applications that developers build on top of Android and iPhone make obvious examples, but many entrepreneurs are using DJI's open application programming interfaces (A.P.I.s) and developer platform to build products on top of DJI's drone to add capabilities and value beyond the basic DJI offering of a flying smartphone. And we may regard Tesla as a software platform attached to a battery and a chassis. While Tesla has not yet opened up its A.P.I., hobbyists have reverse-engineered it, and there is a thriving exchange of modifications. Furthermore, in company with other vehicle manufacturers, Tesla now enjoys numerous aftermarket products made to improve the car in various ways.

Platforms can also be built upon successful applications. Uber is seeking to diversify its revenue stream by basing food delivery and transportation logistics on its very popular ride-hailing app. Google Maps has a fast-growing business selling access to its geospatial information and constant updates to application companies that require maps and other related data.

Other Common Platform Characteristics

For the most part, the key element common to innovation platforms is software, which makes possible the platforms that incorporate the speed and reach they display today. Platform businesses also tend to share three further key characteristics: network effects, distribution power, and asymmetric growth.

Network Effects: The More, the Merrier

Platform businesses enjoy network effects, meaning that every additional user of a platform makes the platform more interesting to sellers and more valuable to both. The higher the number of connected users and of products, services, or pieces of information on a platform, the more valuable it becomes, and the harder to dislodge. Technologies, too, undergo this effect, as the fax machine, the smartphone, and online multiplayer games illustrate. The most valuable platforms tend to have strong network effects. The LinkedIn social network for business, as well as the German competitor XING, become far stronger and more valuable as more people participate in it.

Distribution Power: Lots of Money Goes to Others

Platform business models expand rapidly by enabling other businesses to profit by them. In addition, platform businesses tend to be particularly helpful for so-called long tail transactions and businesses, wherein volume and demand may both be limited. This enables significantly more participants to benefit from them. So, for example, eBay can equally well support someone who sells only a handful of items each month and a large retailer that treats eBay as another fullblown digital sales channel.

Asymmetric Growth and Competition: Giving It Away

Large platform businesses commonly attract customers by giving away a significant subset of some service, either by monetizing the service indirectly with ads or by selling user data. Google and Facebook famously pioneered this using search and social networks respectively, but many platform businesses do it. Apple, for example, enables free distribution of many types of content and many device functions. By giving away something first or foremost, platform companies can rapidly build a customer base large enough to successfully market their commercial products.

Every Company Wants to Be a Platform Company

Though companies with many elements of platform businesses have existed for thousands of years, the phrase *platform business* became more widespread in the early 2000s. Since then, venture capitalists have become infatuated with the model. They love it because it is highly capital efficient and has very low requirements for capital expenditures or purchases of physical goods. Platforms thrive on so-called intangible investments. CEOs love it, too. In survey after survey, senior leaders in numerous industries have expressed a strong desire to develop a platform component in their businesses.

Patagonia used all these advantages to expand from a one-way retail outlet into a marketplace—more fully owning its relationship with customers. In fact, Patagonia is itself using a platform company, Trove (formerly Yerdle), to support its online reselling. Nested platforms are common.

Many industries have had vertically integrated marketplaces for some time. Apple, for instance, has long accepted trade-ins and sold reconditioned items, and car dealerships have, since time immemorial, purchased and resold used cars as incentive to upgrade to newer vehicles.

But key changes have made marketplaces easier to create and to modernize. Today, everyone who opens a smartphone is shopping. Search engines have made it far easier for shoppers to find marketplaces and for marketplaces to advertise to the right shoppers—particularly to those who already show shopping intent, as is the genius of Google's powerful AdWords technologies. This greatly facilitates finding and recruiting potential users of products at the prototype stage, when designers and engineers need to test their products.

Marketplaces and Platforms Are at the Center of Many Innovation Breakthroughs

These interlocking models—marketplaces and platforms—exemplify the many uses of newer technologies in creating businesses that grow more lucrative over time by serving as bases for other businesses. Of course, some of the most innovative businesses are not marketplaces: SpaceX and Dollar Shave Club are not. But all are adopting marketplace characteristics. SpaceX, for instance, is looking to pursue an auction for freight space on its launches; Dollar Shave Club is including additional products and promotions in its boxes. Tesla is expanding beyond cars into other items and has plans to make entertainment offerings via its car systems. Almost any popular business can take on elements of a platform and a marketplace if it determines what parts of its business can be shared, resold, repurposed, or built onto.

Innovative Companies Work Hard on Platform Design

The smartest businesses treat the embrace of platforms as a key to their success rather than as happenstance. Legacy organizations such as farm-equipment maker John Deere and industrial conglomerate General Electric are dabbling in marketplace and platform business models with a view to unlocking new and additional revenues, and they embrace wholeheartedly the new opportunities that exponential technologies create. Moreover, they are willing to recognize that perhaps they do not know what the next great business model will be.

Programming Amazon to Be a Platform-Making Company

This is, in part, why Amazon has famously enforced its A.P.I. manifesto: all internal businesses shall build software routines, protocols, and tools that all users can access and use to build their own businesses on top of or alongside. This is the genius of Amazon Web Services, which began as an internal I.T. project and has since become Jeff Bezos's most prolific profit center. This will be particularly critical as A.I. and quantum computing reduce the cost of many fields of information processing, making their application newly affordable to various problems and services.

The power of platforms is very well explained in a book, *Platform Revolution: How Networked Markets Are Transforming the Economy and How to Make Them Work for You,* by Geoffrey Parker, Marshall Van

Alstyne, and Sangeet Choudary, who show how platform businesses bring together producers and consumers in high-value exchanges in which the chief assets are information and interactions.[2] These interactions are the creators of value, the sources of competitive advantage. It is the interactions that give Silicon Valley advantages over competitors in every industry.

Platforms are ushering in a new business environment, in which a handful of powerful businesses are becoming more dominant than ever. They are also becoming more vulnerable, though, to changing sentiments, customer tastes, and technological obsolescence, and the ability to create platform models and related innovations relies heavily on a workplace culture to foster it—which we'll explore further in the next chapter.

10

How to (Dis)organize for Innovation

CHAPTER SUMMARY: DeWALT created a runaway success with an elegant but simple innovation in batteries, increasing annual revenue by hundreds of millions of dollars. We discuss the importance to innovation of reducing friction, ensuring that top management spends time talking with employees and customers close to the ground and creating ways that teams and people with new ideas can be heard, nurtured, and valued even if their ideas don't pan out. We include a decreasing innovation friction checklist to assist in identifying what may be obstructing innovation in an organization.

Innovation is not served by perfect organization or confinement to a program but by a little unpredictability, such as arises in talking with customers or in serendipitous meetings with other units. This is precisely why Apple's Steve Jobs designed both the Pixar Studios building and the new Apple campus in Cupertino to foster frequent random encounters between employees by (among other approaches) making them walk past each other as they crossed the campus and ate together in a cafeteria. Enforcing this does not guarantee innovation, but it is a necessary condition: randomness and external focus are disorganizing forces requisite for shaking old ways of thinking enough to foster novel thoughts and concepts. In this chapter, we will cover the principles of "dis-organization" and provide some examples of how it has worked in the real world.

DeWALT Helps Construction Unplug

In the United States, one of the most trusted brands of construction tools is that of DeWALT, a subsidiary of Stanley Black & Decker, an industrial conglomerate with $14 billion in 2018 sales. DeWALT has earned the trust of contractors and other tradespeople who use its saws, drills, and other tools by acting on close observation of their customers' use of them, spending a lot of time on job sites, asking about problems that construction teams experience.

On a number of these visits, DeWALT's research teams noticed that contractors favored using cordless, battery-driven drills and saws but remained tethered to generators or the mains in using higher-power tools such as miter saws. The research team saw in this problem a revenue opportunity to market a more powerful battery that could supply both 20 volts, for smaller tools, and 60 volts, for heavier-duty ones. A project team presented the idea to DeWALT senior management, which has a history of experimentation and bottom-up innovation.

Fresh on the heels of a successful innovation using Bluetooth in batteries to track tool locations, DeWALT's senior managers embraced the idea and greenlit product development, and, in 2016, DeWALT introduced its Flexvolt line of adjustable-voltage batteries. The new product line won rave reviews from contractors, and *Popular Science* magazine counted it one of the greatest ten home innovations of the year.[1] By 2018, the Flexvolt line was earning annual revenues of $300 million; and, on the back of that, DeWALT launched other lines of tools requiring greater power or battery life, such as electric lawnmowers.

DeWALT's success was not its first; nor was it an accident. The company's long history of innovative product development arises from both the bottom and the top. It results from Stanley Black & Decker's enforcement of many of the key principles that we believe are essential for (dis)organizing for innovation. Its commitment to innovation is holistic, and the firm's venture arm invests in innovative startups and runs two accelerator programs, in Atlanta and Silicon Valley, in partnership with the leading venture incubator Techstars.

DeWALT provides its innovators with many means of potential support for their ideas, no matter where they live in the company hierarchy. Perhaps most importantly, senior management spends considerable time and energy interacting with innovators and learning what is happening on the ground. "The innovation strategy is globally distributed and diverse, yet holistic and seamlessly integrated into our businesses." Mark Maybury, Stanley Black & Decker's chief technology officer, told the magazine *Strategy+Business* in 2018.[2] From this mass of innovation efforts comes an ethos of (dis)organization: many, many ways to achieve innovation with lots of small bets but no "bet-the-farm" plays.

Creating Innovation by Reducing Friction and Removing Barriers

Available to any organization are several ways in which to nurture and protect innovation.

Encouraging ideas to come from workers at all levels is one that we've covered extensively already. In order to attract ideas in the service of a greater goal, organizations have used digital suggestion boxes, regular team meetings focusing on improving processes, and companywide competitions. The idea for descaling aircraft toilets came through a British Airways companywide idea competition to attain a 50 percent reduction in carbon emissions by 2050. The airline was also the first to contract for plant-based jet fuel.

Another way to encourage innovation is to create small, diverse, interdisciplinary teams. Amazon exemplifies the ability of small teams to foster huge achievements; most of the new business lines at Amazon have emerged from small project teams of no more than a dozen. (Amazon limits team size on the "pizza model"—the notion that a team of more people than can share a couple of pizzas is too large.) Setting very bold goals that you can measure and judge (without worrying if the goals are not met the first time) is the core of the Google OKR (Objectives Key Results) model, where employees are encouraged to shoot for the stars—and are considered successful if they achieve even 70 percent of their goals.

Critical to enabling teams and employees to innovate is allowing them the autonomy to do so. Innovation cannot be scheduled, planned, or mandated; it does not work on a clock or a quarterly calendar; it is not assisted by employee-performance reviews. Because everyone loves to play the innovation game, "feedback" and mentorship from well-intended "experts" higher up in the company easily create time sinks.

Another aid to your internal innovators is to minimize external noise and organizational inertia: to shield them from bureaucracy, meetings, and obligations that are not contributing to their goal; to *not* mandate performance reviews; and to let them avoid death by review committee.

Checklist: Decreasing Innovation Friction

There is no consistently best answer to the questions below; their function is to stimulate thought on the innovation environment.

- ❐ Can a team conceive and launch an innovation project quickly (in a few months or less)?
- ❐ Are your innovation project teams multi-disciplinary?

- ❒ Are people working on innovation projects excused from all the duties of their regular jobs?
- ❒ How frequently are innovation projects expected to make formal reports?
- ❒ How many meetings with project outsiders in each quarter must innovation projects attend in order to provide updates?
- ❒ Do innovation project teams have to go through the same procedures to procure equipment or services as the rest of the company does?
- ❒ Are innovation projects allowed to freely collaborate with external parties?
- ❒ Are innovation projects' members allowed to form a startup to continue their work if the company decides not to pursue the idea?

This may sound like advocacy for an "innovation unit" inside a company, but it has key differences precisely because it occurs from the bottom up rather than from the top down. Sometimes that may even appear to be irresponsible and against the rules. So be it. The teams need to feel urgency and agency, and to have authority and creativity.

Most important of all is to make clear that you expect these entrepreneurs and innovators to fly away and launch their own companies based on ideas incubated in house. This is normal and natural. Taking a restrictive approach to intellectual property will only cause bitterness and will encourage employees to hoard their ideas. Given their wings, some may choose to grow their ideas within the walls of the legacy company; others may feel the need to build something new from the ground up. Either is good, because it builds the brand and reputation, and ideally a new business line or model, while cementing the culture of innovation.

11

The Tactics of Innovative Companies

CHAPTER SUMMARY: This chapter covers tactics that companies, large and small, are using to foster innovation. There are many such tactics, and broadly speaking they include innovation prizes and contests, design sprints, crowdfunding, lean methodologies, borrowing, and recruiting rule breakers and dreamers.

There are many paths to innovation and many viable ways to encourage employees and stakeholders to come up with novel products, solutions, and services. In this chapter, we cover what we consider some of the most viable and well-trialed systems and methodologies applicable directly in an organization, without necessarily spending a lot of money or instituting changes difficult to undo.

Innovation Prizes and Contests

The Ansari XPRIZE was conceived and launched in 1996 to foster innovation in space launches and space flight. The $10 million prize was to be awarded to the first team that could "Build a reliable, re-usable, privately financed, manned spaceship capable of carrying three people to 100 kilometers above the Earth's surface twice within two weeks." This contest launched innovation in affordable, efficient suborbital space flight. It also captured the imagination and attention of a generation of leading engineers. Won by pioneering aerospace entrepreneur Burt Rutan with backing from Microsoft billionaire Paul Allen on October 4, 2004, the XPRIZE made clear that space flight was a field ripe for innovation despite the heavy presence of such established incumbents as Boeing and Arianespace. The relatively small price of this first XPRIZE contest unlocked many billions of dollars in finance.

Another classic, wildly successful innovation challenge was the DARPA Grand Challenge. In the United States, the Defense Advanced Research Projects Administration (DARPA) has initiated a series of scientific challenges that have attracted top research teams from academia and industry. The first DARPA Grand Challenge, with a $1 million prize, held on March 13, 2004, in the Mojave Desert of the United States, was a race to see which autonomous vehicle could travel the greatest distance along a defined route. None of the robot vehicles completed the route, and the winning entrant, from Carnegie Mellon University, traveled only 11.78 kilometers (7.32 miles) of the course before becoming stuck. Later races expanded to cross-country jaunts and then to drones. The teams and researchers involved went on to form the backbone of many of the leading autonomous vehicle efforts that are powering driverless car innovation around the world.

Less prestigious and ambitious contests too can effectively attract innovation and even new products. In the United Kingdom, the government's Innovate UK portal offers money to finance product development and prototypes to companies and groups solving specific problems. For example, one prize posted offered an opportunity "for businesses to apply for a share of £1.08 million, plus VAT, to develop solutions to detect and deter trespass at railway platform ends and edges."[1] Innovate UK has attracted dozens of bids for funding to solve problems that various government agencies in transportation, defense, and health care have raised.

Innovation contests can also work well for small, arguably mundane innovations. For example, what are new uses for duct tape? ShurTech, the owners of the Duck Tape brand of duct tape (an umbrella term for a tape style originally used for affixing insulation and making repairs to pipes and ducts and serving as something of a Swiss Army knife for anything requiring adhesion), has become legendary for running hilarious contests in which consumers show off unexpected uses for duct tape. Contest examples have included a "Stuck at Prom" contest, in which U.S. high-school students designed clothing for the "prom," a popular end-of-year dance event.[2] ShurTech gave away a $10,000 college scholarship to the winner. The original maker of duct tape, 3M, runs its own contests on the Instructables websites, and some of the contests' products have been astounding; a working duct-tape kayak and a lawn chair are two examples. Besides increasing product consumption, such whimsical contests spread ideas on product usage, for just a few thousand dollars.

Innovation contests are not limited to product development; innovation prizes can also foster marketing efforts, rewarding the best campaign ideas, the most compelling videos, the funniest advertisements, the best time-saving idea, and many others. This contest ethos directly affirms that everyone is a potential innovator and inventor.

Design Thinking and Design Sprints

Design firms such as IDEO, Frog Design, and Fjord have long been pioneers in building products that reflect user needs and wants. That aim, often overlooked by in-house teams building products in isolation, is one that design thinking, originating in the 1990s, addresses directly.

As summarized by IDEO, "Design thinking is a process for creative problem solving" with a human-centric approach. It lays out a system and approach for focusing design efforts through listening to the people for whom they are creating. This leads to better products and services, and also tends to clarify and streamline internal processes. Design thinking has also been applied in software development, in what's called the *agile methodology*, wherein every major part of a team's work is broken down into discrete components and described as a "user story" through the eyes of the user. As IDEO explains on its educational website IDEO U: "When you sit down to create a solution for a business need, the first question should always be what's the human need behind it?"[3] Design thinking uses simple tools—whiteboards, pens, paper—to create an inclusive process that puts technical and nontechnical workers on an even footing.

One of the most common ways to apply design thinking is design sprints. A low-cost program originating at Google in 2010, design sprints focuses on putting a client's team into the shoes of a targeted customer or buyer to design and test a new product for that buyer within a week. Design sprints is low tech (paper and pens) and low risk; its client's primary cost is its participating team's time. Google even uses its own service: GV (formerly Google Ventures), Google's venture-capital arm, has a design sprints team that assists funded startups in idea development.

Design sprints in action are a blast. On Day 1, the team defines and maps the problem. On Day 2, individual participants sketch out ideas for solutions. On Day 3, the group votes or decides on which sketches have the greatest potential. On Day 4, the team (sometimes with help) builds a realistic a prototype—which can be as simple as a series of drawings on a legal pad to simulate an iPhone app or as sophisticated as a 3D printed part or even a prototype piece of software. On Day 5, teams test that prototype with five target customers and gather feedback to understand whether their proposed product will resonate with them.

Many notable technology companies and brands use design sprints, including Airbnb, Dropbox, Facebook, Google, LEGO, McKinsey, Medium, *The New York Times,* Slack, and Uber.

The design sprint is not just low risk and efficient; it also serves to take a team out of its usual office work and environment and empowers it to solve a challenging problem and exercise its members' minds in unexpected ways. These tend to be heavily visual, with participants drawing their ideas. Design sprints also level hierarchies usefully; one of the charges of a design sprint's leader is to make sure that everyone contributes and that everyone's contribution is equally valued.

Crowdfunding

In November 2017, the well-regarded German audio electronics concern Bose did something strange: it launched a crowdfunding campaign on the popular crowdfunding site Indiegogo, seeking to raise $50,000 to cover the costs of prototyping a new type of sound-masking earbuds. A pair of these, fitted into the ears, would help users go to sleep.

The campaign went on to raise more than $450,000 in contributions from more than 2,900 backers (whose backing effectively prepurchased the prototype earbuds). The campaign in reality was far less about fundraising than about product validation: confirming that the idea had legs and a real market. Additionally, Bose's product team was able to recruit a large audience of energized, responsive participants into the project, giving Bose a high volume of high-quality feedback. Data and insights gathered from the project eventually led to a second version of the product, which hit the market in late 2018 and is still available today. Those who purchased the original, prototype devices received free upgrades to the production version.

A growing number of organizations are using crowdfunding sites to economically test a product concept on a large audience and to simultaneously test their marketing messages for social selling, email marketing, and other types of campaigns requisite to selling via non-traditional but influential online outlets. The benefits of crowdfunding campaigns are many. Cheaper and offering stronger verification than focus groups, they often present a strong marketing opportunity to attain brand recognition. The fast timetables required enforce innovation discipline in legacy companies' teams. The Bose project, for instance, took a single year, a relatively brisk period for launching a new electronics product.

Lean Methodologies

Popularized by entrepreneurs Steve Blank and Eric Ries, the "lean startup" is a way for innovative businesses to attenuate development cycles and quickly learn whether a proposed business model is viable.[4] Its premise is that startup companies that work to iteratively build products or services designed to solve problems for early customers can minimize market risks and wastage of money on untested feature development and expensive product launches that have not yet been validated as meeting customer needs. Blank and Ries espouse a number of simple ways to test product ideas and get feedback quickly and effectively, without spending a lot of money on technology or focus panels. The goal is to get to a viable product and revenue stream as quickly as possible with minimal risk.

Ries and Blank initially applied this perspective to startups to increase their prospects of commercial success. Its principles have since been applied to innovation processes inside companies of all sizes, not just for new products but also as a way to solve problems. In that sense, the lean startup is closely related to design thinking, but it entails a more drawn-out process.

Borrowing Liberally and Literally

If you are not borrowing ideas from competitors or others, then you are not doing your job. We are not advocating stealing intellectual property or commercial secrets, but rather smart copying and learning from competitors, applying their best offerings to your own products and services.

Silicon Valley succeeds because it excels in sharing ideas and building on the work of others. As Steve Jobs said in 1994, "Picasso had a saying: 'Good artists copy, great artists steal, and we have, you know, always been shameless about stealing great ideas.'"[5] Almost every Apple product has features that were first developed by others; rarely do its technologies wholly originate within the company. The iPod, for example, was invented by British inventor Kane Kramer; iTunes was built on SoundJam MP, a technology purchased from Casady & Greene; and the iPhone frequently copies Samsung's mobile technologies, and vice versa.

Mark Zuckerberg also built Facebook by taking pages from Myspace and Friendster, and he continues to copy others' products. Facebook Places is a replica of Foursquare; Messenger video imitates Skype; Facebook Stories is a clone of Snapchat; and Facebook Live combines the best features of Meerkat and Periscope. Facebook tried mimicking WhatsApp but couldn't gain market share, so it spent a fortune purchasing the company. This is another one of Silicon Valley's methods: if stealing doesn't work, then buy the company.

There is no shame in copying. Innovation smartly borrowed and used to a new end works just as well as innovation arising from within, so teams should recognize that their best idea may be a better version of their competitor's or partner's idea.

Recruiting Rulebreakers and Dreamers

Just as critical as these tactics is capturing the interest of the innovators in your midst. Often the best innovators may not look like the most productive employees. The director of the groundbreaking Pixar Studios feature animation *Incredibles 2,* Brad Bird, heard from nearly everyone at the studio that the movie he wanted to make would be technologically impossible.[6] One of the biggest challenges was to realistically depict flowing hair, and computer graphics systems at the time could not make animated hair lifelike. So Bird sought out employees who were dissatisfied with their roles at Pixar (though not with the company itself). From these people he formed a flock of black sheep who were told to break the rules and just solve the big problems—like flowing hair—without reference to established methods. Identifying and unleashing the yearning to do something better, Pixar created an entirely new way of doing animation, not to mention the highest-grossing animation film series in the history of cinema. Recognizing who might be innovators and offering them the chance and the space to "think different" is just as important as deploying the latest models of innovation. Some people just want to innovate. Finding them and setting them free can pay disproportionate dividends.

12

Change Management and Company Culture: An Innovation Manifesto

CHAPTER SUMMARY: This chapter lays out our innovation manifesto and considers how leaders and managers need to adjust their thinking to empower change at their companies or organizations. To stimulate debate and thought on the topic, we include several checklists about the state of the organization's or company's culture as it relates to innovation.

The Birth of Amazon Prime

In 2004, an Amazon engineer named Charlie Ward dropped an idea into the companywide digital employee suggestion box. This box was an open invitation to all employees to pitch ideas to improve the business. Ward's idea was simple yet provocative: offer free rapid shipping to customers who paid an annual fee. This new program would be a radical and risky departure from Amazon's policy on free shipping on orders over $25, but Ward thought this might induce people to shop more often and spend more money.

Amazon CEO Jeff Bezos, who regularly reads employee improvement suggestions, found the idea compelling. He gathered a group of executives in November 2004 at the boathouse of his home near Seattle, Washington, and told them they had to come up with a proposal to make this new shipping policy viable before Amazon's upcoming earnings call at the end of January 2005.[1] As Greg Greeley, an Amazon executive who was present at the meeting, told *The Seattle Times* in 2015, "We knew we were building something that was going to be new and different. We knew we were onto something."

Thus was born Amazon Prime, in February 2005. Logistics experts doubted that Amazon could cover the shipping bills. But Amazon Prime attracted tens of thousands of customers within a few months, each paying a $79 annual fee. In the spring of 2018, Amazon exceeded 100 million Prime users, who are contributing an annual company revenue of $10 billion through their (now $99) annual Prime subscriptions alone.[2] Prime has also become, just as Ward envisioned, an incredibly "sticky" way to get shoppers to make Amazon their default purchase option.

Bezos is now preparing Prime to accelerate delivery from two-day to same-day delivery of most products. "Customers love the transition of Prime from two days to one day—they've already ordered billions of items with free one-day delivery this year. It's a big investment, and it's the right long-term decision for customers," Bezos said during a company earnings call in the summer of 2019.[3]

Since Prime's inception, Amazon has used it as a way to improve and better tune its supply-chain logistics and warehouse systems on several key fronts: keeping better track of where any given item might be in Amazon's warehouses, calculating the best path by which to get it to a Prime subscriber, and then taking best advantage of an ad hoc delivery network involving several providers and, as increasingly is the case, Amazon's own logistics capabilities. Now, Amazon is building a full-blown logistics business, with dozens of planes and thousands of trucks. This business is likely to become, in the near future, yet another business unit selling its services to the outside, in keeping with Bezos's mandate to design any internal service in such a way that external businesses can become its customers.

The Lesson from Prime: Give Employees Permission to Innovate

Prime might have happened anyway; but the way it did come about shows how key management practices can have a disproportionate effect on innovation. To change the trajectory of the standard legacy company and allow that company to envision a transformation to newer and better business models, CEOs and leaders must give employees permission to innovate, considering the possibility that each one of their workers has the potential for a billion-dollar idea.

This has long been the approach of Japanese manufacturers, which have created some of the most recession-proof, well-run, innovative manufacturing businesses on the planet (carmaker Toyota being the epitome). In Japanese manufacturing, management seriously evaluates any suggestion for process or product improvement from anyone, from a junior laborer to a senior vice president.

This openness is the core of what has made Toyota such a resilient business. Curiously, such openness has also resulted in lucrative business lines in some of the most notable technology companies. We've already mentioned the example of 3M. Google's Gmail began as a so-called 20 percent project, an exploratory effort that Google expressly permitted by awarding its engineers 20 percent of their work week to pursue any project. Gmail has since become a multi-billion-dollar business line for the search giant.

Small Innovation Ideas Can Add Up Quickly

Innovation and ideas do not, though, need to be enormous in order to be useful; that's the beauty of fostering a culture of innovation and ideation. For example, British Airways, which also runs a digital suggestion box and closely monitors ideas, received a simple idea that saved nearly $1 million per year in costs: to descale (or aggressively clean) toilet pipes on planes.[4] This reduced the weight of the planes and, by extension, reduced fuel costs. Descaling pipes was one of 200 ideas submitted. Not all the ideas were implemented, but implementing the descaling idea, along with a handful of others, resulted in the airline's reducing costs by $20 million per year.

A digital suggestion box is a great first step. A senior manager must read the suggestions, acknowledge them, and personally thank their submitters. And it's equally important that suggestions and improvements be celebrated and lauded, as employees must feel that the ideas they contribute will be considered and honored.

That may sound impracticable for a company of a size such as Amazon's today, with hundreds of thousands of employees. But it is critical to keep listening, companywide, even on such an enormous scale. It must be a usual frame of mind and a continual practice, not a one-off during an annual innovation contest or idea festival. From this simple mindset change can grow more radical changes; a broader embrace of risk-taking; and a corporate culture giving employees permission, space, and encouragement to innovate.

An Innovation Manifesto and Mindset for Change

With that in mind, we lay out a manifesto for creating a corporate culture that fosters innovation.

Great ideas can come from anywhere, so provide for them to come by assuming that everyone is an innovator. Many know the origin story of the Post-It Note at 3M, a runaway product success created by a company chemist named Spencer Silver. What's less well known is the overall effect of 3M's innovation program. 3M has 22,800 patents. Many of those patents come from ideas generated during that program.

This inclusive innovation effort is not a secondary component of 3M's enduring success. As Kurt Beinlich, a technical director for 3M, told *Fast Company*, "It's really shaped what and who 3M is."[5] 3M is a company founded in 1902 in Minnesota as the Minnesota Mining and Manufacturing Company. Today, it is one of the world's leading industrial manufacturing companies, with tens of thousands of products. It has remained relevant and innovative by constantly embracing change, trying new products and ideas, and expanding into new markets.

In fact, it goes deeper than this. A growing body of research indicates that home inventors contribute massively to economic growth and new product initiatives. According to MIT innovation scholar Eric von Hippel, "In just six countries surveyed to date, tens of millions of individuals in the household sector have been found to collectively spend tens of billions of dollars in time and materials per year developing products for their own use." According to surveys by von Hippel and others, more than 5 percent of the U.S. population is engaged in some form of creative invention or innovation.[6]

Von Hippel believes, despite Joseph Schumpeter's widely accepted innovation thesis that scientists and researchers are the most common sources of innovation, that home inventors and everyday innovators make a far larger contribution to economic development than was previously understood. Because this inventive work is not measured unless it results in an actual company selling products or services, economists cannot easily place a value on their economic activity. Increasingly, these home innovations spill over into the commercial realm and become entirely new product categories and industries.[7]

An example that von Hippel cites is the mountain-bike industry. A group of cyclists began to experiment by riding beach cruisers equipped with fat tires down the sides of hills in Marin County, California. Riding a bike down a mountain required stronger brakes, a stiffer frame, and shock absorbers on the wheel forks and seat posts. For years, bike manufacturers refused to acknowledge the nascent sport, and even complained about it, saying that this was not the way to treat a bike and that the mountain-bike pioneers were violating warranties. It was not until tens of thousands of people had jury-rigged mountain bikes and an underground industry was thriving that major bike manufacturers decided to take part. Today, there are tens of millions of mountain-bike riders in the United States, and the industry pulls in billions of dollars in annual sales—none of which would be likely save for the efforts of some stubborn, fun-loving backyard inventors.

Checklist: Making Everyone an Innovator

- ❒ How does your company give every employee a chance to innovate?
- ❒ Do you have formal innovation programs and opportunities open to employees to realize their ideas?
- ❒ Do you offer employees any time during the year to work on new ideas they may have generated?
- ❒ Does your company have a digital suggestion box or internal social media-type discussion network that is well publicized? Does senior management read those suggestions?
- ❒ Do you have examples to hand out of products, features, or services whose origins lie beyond the product, design, and engineering teams?
- ❒ Do you have a formal recognition program for great ideas or successful innovation projects?

The future of company innovation, then, may be to tap into these backyard inventors when they are on their day jobs. The idea factory does not turn off merely because one is inventing for others; inventive people solve problems as part of their nature. So, for legacy companies to innovate and succeed as their startups do, they need to treat their people as Google, Toyota, 3M, and British Airways treat their workers: as founts of ideas. They must recognize that entrepreneurship is only a state of mind and does not depend on age, skin color, sex, or background. Following logically along this path, companies that want to chase exponential innovation and massive self-transformation must facilitate and motivate employee activities in innovation and ideation.[8] This cannot be window-dressing. At Toyota, it's the regular team meetings. At 3M, it's the idea fairs. At Amazon, it's the constant tending of the digital suggestion box. At Google, it's the ability to float a product idea and recruit a small team to work on a prototype with few barriers. We cannot stress too much that treating everyone as an innovator is the most basic and essential part of building an innovation culture that works. It is essential to an organization of any size, but it is particularly so to larger and older companies that have rigid, ingrained hierarchies and communication structures.

Motivate, Facilitate, Collaborate: Coaches, Not Bosses

The days of rigid work hierarchies are gone. Workers, for their part, hate hierarchies, and so do most CEOs. Smart CEOs understand that enforced hierarchies separate them from what is really going on in the company or organization, often to their detriment or peril, and they know that they're more effective helping, supporting, and partnering than merely directing from on high.

Coach and Motivate

These skills can be encapsulated in the phrase "coaches, not bosses" Bosses are prescriptive and definitive. Coaches question and listen, asking workers to come up with their own answers and guiding them rather than telling them. This approach, however—and even the ability to follow it—remains in a minority. In a study conducted by academic Julia Milner and leadership expert Trenton Milner that focused on testing managers' management and coaching styles, the researchers found that "when initially asked to coach, many managers instead demonstrated a form of consulting. Essentially, they simply provided the other person with advice or a solution. We regularly heard comments like, 'First you do this' or 'Why don't you do this?'"[9]

This was a relatively small study, but our experience in observing management in many old-school companies sadly suggests that it represents the norm. It probably didn't work well when employees used to be less mobile and less willing to quit their jobs. It certainly doesn't work now, when workers are far less loyal to their companies than they were in the past and the companies are competing for skilled workers more than skilled workers are competing for their jobs.

Telling knowledge workers (or even manufacturing and service workers) how to do their jobs results in unhappy workers. Yes, training is necessary. Yes, continuing education is vital. But there's a tremendous difference in delivery and approach between *telling* and *teaching.*

Facilitate

Facilitation works hand in hand with motivation: it is far easier to motivate engaged employees who feel well supported. Employees crave learning, in fact. In 2018, Facebook's talent management team compared data they had collected on employees who left within the following six months with data on those who stayed. The workers who had chosen to remain at Facebook "found their work enjoyable 31 percent more often, used their strengths 33 percent more often, and expressed 37 percent more confidence that they were gaining the skills and experiences they need to develop their careers."[10]

Collaborate

Collaboration is the third pillar. Legacy companies too often divide themselves internally by department or function. This stifles innovation. Creating a company environment that lubricates collaboration between employees on interesting work is what leads to serendipity and great ideas. We think better and can solve problems more efficiently in collaboration. The movie studio Pixar, which has produced an unprecedented string of successes, is a practitioner of totally open collaboration channels. Its then CEO Ed Catmull described it in this way:

> Members of any department should be able to approach anyone in another department to solve problems without having to go through "proper" channels. It also means that managers need to learn that they don't always have to be the first to know about something going on in their realm, and it's OK to walk into a meeting and be surprised. The impulse to tightly control the process is understandable given the complex nature of moviemaking, but problems are almost by definition unforeseen.

The most efficient way to deal with numerous problems is to trust people to work out the difficulties directly with each other without having to check for permission.[11]

Furthermore, a diversity of viewpoints helps collaboration yield ideas that are more creative and have more economic advantages than those emerging from monocultures.

It's important to note that collaboration does not mean the classic "brainstorming" model: putting everyone in a room and asking them to come up with ideas, no negativity or criticism allowed. Researchers found out 50 years ago that this model for innovation actually produces fewer good ideas than allowing individuals to brainstorm alone. Brainstorming is more effective when individuals brainstorm separately and then come back together to assess ideas. This helps overcome the tendency for the loudest voices in the room to dominate the discussion.[12] Facilitated brainstorming, which is part of Google's innovative Design Thinking program, can be effective in group settings. Incorporating visual elements (such as drawing ideas) is another technique that can improve brainstorming and, by extension, collaborative ideation.

Checklist: Motivate, Facilitate, Collaborate

- ❒ Has your company embraced new collaboration techniques such as design thinking?
- ❒ What does your company do to train employees in communication skills?
- ❒ Does your company have a meeting protocol to ensure efficient and fair meetings?
- ❒ Has it instituted any collaboration processes?
- ❒ What training does it offer managers to help them better motivate employees?
- ❒ Is it regularly running surveys to understand employees' motivations and perceptions of their work?
- ❒ Do employees feel comfortable approaching and speaking with senior managers?
- ❒ How accessible are senior managers to regular employees?
- ❒ Can the company point to any specific successful innovation projects that have emerged from collaboration?
- ❒ How much of company employees' time is spent working in cross-functional teams?
- ❒ Do the employees self-segregate by unit and function at lunch and in other social settings?
- ❒ Is the physical office space designed to foster collaboration?

Empower and Experiment

No one can be innovative without some sense of agency and selfdetermination. The best ideas never emerge from originators who feel powerless in their roles. So smarter companies chasing innovation must give employees and managers the power to step up and try things quickly and independently. This may mean that they can circumvent procurement rules or buy ads on the fly to test a concept on Google or hire a videographer or a programmer in a more streamlined fashion: that they be able to follow their natural tendencies to figure out solutions to problems and test their products. In enabling innovative employees and managers to plot their own course, the company must ask that in return they experiment and move as quickly as possible.

It is possible to remove their fear of failure by making clear that failure means not that they have made a mistake, but they haven't tried enough times yet. To build a culture of experimentation that shrugs off failure and congratulates success, the company can hire entrepreneurs to come and work as intrapreneurs; give them one-year contracts; and ask them to build a product, letting them show your team how it can be done on the outside and helping them get it done in the same way on the inside. The reeducation and experimentation process may take a long time, but cultures cannot be replaced wholesale at a push of a button, as making employees familiar with and fluent in entrepreneurship and innovation can take years. This makes paramount the need for a firm, public, demonstrable commitment by the powers that be.

Checklist: Empowerment and Experimentation

- ❐ How does your company empower its employees and managers to innovate?

- ❐ Does it provide employees with space or time to pursue new ideas and self-directed work?
- ❐ What incentives does your company offer employees to undertake ideation and come up with new solutions?
- ❐ How does your company signal that experimentation is acceptable?
- ❐ What clear criteria does it provide for an innovation project's success?
- ❐ Is it able to identify real examples of experimentation inside the organization?
- ❐ When a project fails, what happens to the team?
- ❐ How do senior managers participate in the experimentation process?
- ❐ Do the experimentation teams have access to internal and external expertise for domain-specific problems?

13

How to Recognize and Use the Strengths of Incumbency

CHAPTER SUMMARY: This chapter covers how incumbent companies are recognizing their strengths and using them to foster innovation and growth. Common incumbent advantages are scale, distribution, data, and expertise: things that are expensive to acquire and difficult for startups to replicate.

Part of what can make effective innovation so powerful inside legacy firms and older organizations is the ability to leverage the existing strengths. We will provide examples of how innovative companies are doing this well and provide some insights and guidance on how you can apply this leverage in your own organization.

Salmon Crisps and Going off the Eaten Path at Sainsbury's

In November 2019, Danone bid adieu to Ayem, a breakfast-bowl product studded with almonds and healthy omega 3 oils.[1] The product had been part of Danone's efforts to break into the fast-growing functional food market. It was the first product to emerge from the Danone incubator, an internal innovation bureau mandated to produce real products and engaging brands to meet burgeoning consumer needs.[2] With a small team of scientists, marketers, and brand experts, Ayem launched in a fraction of the time usually required by the food giant to place a new product on the shelves. When Ayem didn't gain traction after a year, Danone shut it down and cut its losses.

Undeterred, Danone's incubator is launching several other internally incubated food brands, including an allergy-friendly snack line that allows parents to customize their snack purchases to prevent their children's exposure to potentially harmful allergens. Another Danone incubator product, a glass-jarred chic chocolate-ganache dessert called Pati & Coco, landed in the market and graced the shelves of the United Kingdom's second-largest grocer, Sainsbury's, in a distribution and new-product partnership.[3]

This is where Sainsbury's own Future Brands innovation team took up the baton. Launched in April 2018, Future Brands, a small unit inside the supermarket giant, identifies, recruits, and nurtures new brands in any category, including groceries, drinks, cosmetics, and gifts. In exchange for helping them get placement in Sainsbury's, Future Brands asks for a limited period of exclusivity in major supermarket distribution. In the summer of 2019, Future Brands launched a "Taste of the Future" program, which gives customers the chance to try 30 products in the first U.K. supermarkets to offer them. Products include alcoholic kombucha Bootleg Booch, and Sea Chips, a new variety of salmon-skin crisps. With 27 million customers, Sainsbury's is one of the premiere placement options for any food or beverage brand in all of Europe, let alone the United Kingdom.

What Sainsbury's seeks to benefit from is the increasing willingness of shoppers to try new brands and new products—which is especially relevant in the realm of tastes. The Future Brands team represents a wide range of internal disciplines, from buying and marketing to brand and strategy. The diversity is designed to help these small brands navigate Sainsbury's systems and tackle any internal barriers. The team also hires several external specialists with expertise in marketing smaller brands. "We're here to support the business to be a bit bolder and take a few more risks going into the areas we believe will blow up," the unit's head, Rachel Eyre, told *MarketingWeek*.[4] When a brand is selected for stocking at Sainsbury's stores, the Future Brands team creates a marketing and growth plan using data from Sainsbury's Nectar loyalty program to create online marketing, guerrilla campaigns, and in-store spots through which to pump the new products.

More Customers to Watch, More Data to Learn From, More Ways to Try New Things

The basic idea is simple: see what shoppers buy, and utilize data arising from the trial runs of challenger brands to determine which come into demand and which don't. The brands also enjoy an online presence on Sainsburys.co.uk. There is no prescribed end date for the Future Brands arrangements, effectively acknowledging that different brands may require different amounts of time to achieve critical mass. Data from the grocer's Nectar program offer granular detail on brand performance, aiding decision-making.

In addition, the Future Brands team serves as trend spotters for the entire company and often works with other major food companies to bring up-and-coming brands to the United Kingdom. For example, the Future Brands team collaborated with PepsiCo subsidiary Rare Fare Foods to bring the Off the Eaten Path brand of veggie snack foods to shelves in Britain. The team works closely with company buyers, sharing product information and trend information, and it consults with venture-capital firms and accelerators to learn what it is that investors are placing their faith in.

Sainsbury's Future Brands team has the advantage of several strengths of incumbency to stoke sales growth. For example, becausc sales of functional foods and beverages are expected to grow by 8 percent annually,[5] outstripping growth of legacy food items, Future Trends is using its present distribution network, marketing expertise, and sales data to help itself by helping its customers. A startup health-food company distributing, say, kale chips sauteed in pumpkin oil would endure a lengthy, expensive path to reach the shelves of a large supermarket by the usual route. It would first need to convince smaller outlets to stock its wares locally. Having proven the wares' market worth, it would need to secure distribution through a regional distributor. Then it would need to attend major exhibition events for grocery-food buyers in order to gain exposure. Once it succeeded in obtaining a large order, it would need to take out a large line of credit, at high interest rates, for its production runs and print packaging. For Future Brands, Sainsbury's provides distribution and store exposure to customers and also allows the startup brands to gain better rates on production runs of food because the contract factories feel more assured that the product's sales won't fail right away. All told, Future Brands saves both Sainsbury's and its Future Brands partners time, dollars, and stress.

This is a perfect example of how incumbents can use their existing strengths to drive and accelerate innovation. A startup cannot access data from millions of customers, use extant marketing channels, or quickly identify reliable overseas production sources for products. For similar reasons, it cannot readily obtain feedback from a large extant base of users or customers. It must fight for distribution of its products and never has the extent of distribution networks and channels that an incumbent enjoys.

The Many Advantages of Incumbency

As we stated previously, common incumbent advantages are scale, distribution, data, and expertise: things that are expensive to acquire and difficult for startups to replicate. Smarter incumbents are recognizing how to use these advantages to build newer platforms or marketplaces.

As we see with Sainsbury's, incumbent distribution networks and expertise can be valuable to external partners; and the same benefits apply to internal product efforts. Increasingly, companies seek both to engage challenger brands and upstart products and, learning from working with them, to "startupify" some of their own internal new product efforts.

The world's largest beer, wine, and spirits company, Anheuser-Busch InBev (ABInBev), for example, recognized several decades ago that, in the United States, regional microbeers were growing faster and selling at a higher premium than incumbent national beer brands such as Budweiser.

So ABInBev started aggressively buying stakes in these microbeer brands, in part to understand how they marketed themselves and how they crafted stories. In exchange, it plugged the smaller brands into a national distribution channel, giving them unparalleled market access. It also offered production expertise and allowed these beer brands to produce in its large facilities. Often, when the relationship proved sound, ABInBev bought out the entire microbrewery company. ABInBev became so fluent in the microbeer market that it has successfully launched a number of brands that mimic microbeers but are entirely its own creations, such as Shock Top, a Belgian-style brand that is nearly impossible to distinguish from hip microbrews.

Other breweries have followed ABInBev's lead. Dutch brewing giant Heineken bought out all remaining shares in Lagunitas, a well-respected, widely distributed independent U.S. beer brand, in 2017; the two-stage acquisition cost Heineken more than $1 billion. MillerCoors, likewise, both buys microbreweries and launches its own labels.

Large Capital Expenditures Can Be a Weapon Rather Than a Weakness

The story of beer companies also highlights a smart way to take ready advantage of an aversion common to newer business models, venture capitalists, and startups: their aversion to capital expenditures.[6] Few venture capitalists still want to invest in businesses that require major capital investments, because larger investments are perceived as riskier and not as lucrative.

As in the beer market, we are seeing similar stories of large automotive companies smartly working with startups to market their innovations. Cruise Automation, a prominent maker of autonomous-vehicle technology, was purchased by General Motors both because of its technology and because the Cruise team decided that it would rather innovate inside a giant incumbent than go out and raise massive amounts of capital. GM's interaction with Cruise—helpful but at arm's length—has perfectly demonstrated how not to smother a startup acquisition.

The Six Resource Advantages of Legacy Brands

Legacy brands enjoy six significant resource advantages:

1. access to funding
2. access to production and infrastructure
3. access to expertise
4. access to distribution
5. access to data (for A.I. and machine learning)
6. the power of their legacy brands

Any of these six resources can be used to accelerate innovation by themselves. Collectively, they can make innovation truly formidable and can facilitate and accelerate legacy companies' abilities not only to innovate from within but also to quickly increase the production, marketing, and sales of acquired firms.

In the case of ABInBev, craft brewer acquisitions and new internal brands alike were able to tap into several of these established resources: production, distribution, marketing dollars, expertise, and funding.

The one they could not use was brand: in the world of microbreweries, large corporate brewers are the bad guys.

To give you an idea, it often takes a new brewery several years to gain a toehold in shelves and bars in a single city. As soon as ABInBev entered Kona Brewing's Longboard Island Lager into its production and distribution chain, the Hawaii-based brewer could sell beers from San Francisco to New York City without hiring drivers or buying expensive brewing equipment. Selling at prices double or triple those of older, less sought-after beers, Longboard Lager provides ABInBev with much-needed growth in what was a stagnant category.

If we consider the potential for applying A.I. analysis across all the brewing activities undertaken by ABInBev, of all the customer sales data and all the bar consumption data, we get a sense of the potential power of incumbency. With this intelligence, ABInBev could spot seasonal historical trends by product and by individual store and thereby tune distribution strategies to maximum effect; or it could spot trending product flavors and use that insight to focus acquisition strategies or product development.

In an era of exponentially increasing innovation, these resource advantages can be even greater. As we saw it do for Future Brands, access to data and machine-learning capabilities can provide a critical leg up for incumbents. Used in conjunction with the incumbents' marketing reach and marketing expertise in digital promotions such as Google AdWords and Facebook advertising, the power that an incumbent business can wield increases considerably.

Not surprisingly, though, competition for access to these resources is intense. High-quality expertise in any organization is prized, and time with experts becomes a precious resource. Any marketing campaign dedicated to a startup idea or an internal (or external) challenger brand means fewer marketing resources for a legacy product. For this reason, innovations need clear, public executive sponsorship, affording them access to the resources as needed. Companies can achieve that by various means.

Checklist: Incumbent Superpowers

- ❒ Do your organization's innovation projects get ready access to internal domain expertise?
- ❒ Does your organization have a dedicated innovation or experimentation program to ensure that the organization holds resources in reserve to supply innovation efforts?
- ❒ Is your organization's brand a plus or a minus for innovation projects?
- ❒ What variety of people do teams on innovation projects include?
- ❒ How does your organization publicly demonstrate clear support for innovation (excluding window dressing!)?
- ❒ What happens to the leads of innovation projects after they fail? How commonly do they attempt another innovation project?
- ❒ Do innovation projects have full access to any useful data and intelligence gathered by the larger company or organization?
- ❒ What types of innovative marketing strategies do the innovation projects enjoy?

Coca-Cola, which has a track record of terrible failures (e.g., the New Coke), gives internal innovators permission to fail and shows sponsorship by what it calls the Celebrated Failure Award. This award is one of the categories, listed among the great successes, in the company's annual Global Innovator Awards. In 2017, Ali Akbar, a director of sparkling beverages for the firm's Middle East and North Africa business unit, won the prize for an unsuccessful try at launching an energy drink called Sprite 3G in Pakistan to challenge a dominant incumbent.[7]

The resources available chiefly to incumbent companies become advantages only when they are available to innovators and when people at the highest levels of the company are willing to commit time and resources to supporting the innovation. Are you using your legacy resources to best effect?

14

From Dinosaurs to Eagles: Four Case Studies

CHAPTER SUMMARY: This chapter looks at four case studies of innovative companies: Logitech (the world's largest maker of computer peripherals); Microsoft (the world's largest software company); NextEra Energy (the world's largest generator of renewable energy from the sun and wind); and Tech Mahindra—which reinvented itself by focusing on long-term cultural transformation.

Case Study 1: How Logitech Went from Slow Death to Thriving: Design Focus

Logitech's CEO, Bracken Darrell, keeps a copy of the legendary designer Dieter Rams's "Ten Principles for Good Design" on the wall of the conference room next to his open office desk. The German industrial designer is a guru to many of the leading product designers of our time, including Jony Ives of Apple. Darrell, too, believes passionately in the power of design. This belief is what has underlain his execution of a stunning turnaround of his struggling company over the past seven years.

The Logitech that Darrell arrived at in 2012, when he joined as president, was known mostly for cheap computer mice in neutral colors and clunky, forgettable keyboards. The company created products to fit price points and often launched products without significant market testing. At best, the products were uninspired; at worst, they were ugly.

Inspired by Apple as well as by his own experience as President of Procter & Gamble's Braun division, Darrell resolved to reinvent Logitech "as a design company." This seemed a tall order for a maker of black mice and keyboards, and he knew that he would need a design leader as his partner and to build a culture of design excellence before he could pair Logitech's impeccable product engineering and manufacturing with eye-popping design. And that combination, Darrell believed, would turn the company around and make it a lot more exciting to customers, investors, and its own employees.

The alternative was a dark future. Logitech sales had stagnated before Darrell joined. The market for plain PC peripherals was not growing: smartphone and laptop users had no need for them.

Design Principles and Purpose

To effect the transformation, Darrell assigned resources to match his vision. He took two-thirds of the company's $200 million annual R&D budget away from mice and keyboards and used it to place bets on faster-growing sectors. He recruited a very respected designer who had led design at Nokia: Alastair Curtis. The team, now boasting more than 100 designers, has attracted talent from Nike, IDEO, and other leading companies.

To give this transformation a heart and soul, Darrell and Curtis created design principles that echoed those of Dieter Rams. Logitech's principles are simple and elegant:

- *Powerful Idea:* clarity of purpose and the benefit to the consumer
- *Soul:* unique personality of the product/experience

- *Effortless:* relentless pursuit of creating friction-free experiences
- *Crafted:* simplifying, perfecting, and stripping down to the essential
- *Magical:* interactions that are alive and expressive

The idea is not to build products merely to fill a niche, but to build products to fill a need, and to do so in a way that creates emotional resonance and crafts a comfortable, seamless user experience. Having a major unifying idea behind every new product was a powerful way to force designers, marketers, and everyone else working for Logitech to check whether the feature they were designing or the marketing campaign they were planning fitted the unifying idea of the product.

For example, Logitech's Circle Home security streaming-camera system provides a visual principle—the device is circle-shaped—and a language concerning the circle encompassing our homes, our loved ones, and the places we care about and want to watch. Logitech's Spotlight Presentation Pointer is designed to help audiences focus on the speaker. Even in products deriving from Logitech's past, the design teams are striving to add one or two seminal features that improve the lives of their users. On keyboards, for instance, Logitech began adding dials so that people could scroll through menus with their keyboard rather than with an inexact mouse.

Innovation is considered the domain of mathematicians and scientists, and engineering often receives all the focus. But the most important lesson that Steve Jobs taught the tech industry concerned the importance of form. "Design is the fundamental soul of a man-made creation that ends up expressing itself in successive outer layers of the product or service," he said. This is what Darrell also demonstrated: engineering is assuredly important, but what makes a technology product most successful is its design.

An important myth that Darrell helps shatter concerns the backgrounds of people who can make exponential innovations happen: they don't need to be geeks and nerds. This too is something on which Steve Jobs held a very strong opinion. "It's in Apple's DNA that technology alone is not enough—that it's technology married with liberal arts, married with the humanities, that yields us the result that makes our heart sing. And nowhere is that more true than in these post-PC devices," said Jobs at the unveiling of the iPad 2 in March 2011.[1] Darrell himself majored in English at a small liberal arts college in Arkansas before completing an MBA at Harvard.

There are other great liberal arts examples: YouTube's chief executive, Susan Wojcicki, majored in history and literature; Slack's founder, Stewart Butterfield, in English; Airbnb's founder, Brian Chesky, in the fine arts; and, in China, Alibaba's chief executive, Jack Ma, in English. In the new era of converging exponentially advancing technologies, creating the most disruptive solutions often requires a knowledge of fields such as biology, education, health sciences, and human behavior.

Tackling today's greatest social and technological challenges requires the ability to think critically about their human context—something in which humanities graduates happen to be well trained.

Diversifying and Simplifying

The digital-native brands we cited earlier, such as Dollar Shave Club, were the cool kids on the block. They had figured out how to sell directly to customers, bypassing the traditional song and dance of securing distribution and shelf space at a major physical storefront. They played the Amazon merchandising game as if they were born to it, running circles around legacy brands. These digital natives often created market buzz that resonated initially with Millennials and Generation Xers, often expanding then into other demographic age groups. They also tended to refresh products more often and vary their approaches to marketing.

Under Darrell, Logitech accelerated a multi-brand strategy, better utilizing existing assets and, in a few instances, acquiring new ones.

Logitech's UE (Ultimate Ears) brand broke out as a popular Bluetooth speaker brand, winning numerous prestigious awards from audio reviews and tech publications. The company made another key acquisition in 2016 with the purchase of Jaybird, a fast-growing wireless-earbuds company founded by Australian entrepreneur Judd Armstrong. Jaybird had carved out a premium wireless-audio brand with a strong following among athletes and adventure-sports pros. Logitech then went on to acquire two rapidly expanding complementary brands, Blue (microphones) and ASTRO Gaming (gaming headsets).

Darrell's years at large companies had taught him the good and bad of them. On the positive side, they remained disciplined on cost and invested in sales and marketing. On the negative, they could be stiflingly bureaucratic and slow and could kill off entrepreneurship and innovation as business grew. Darrell kept teams small and independent, to maintain the feeling of a small company, and he flattened the organization, having more than twenty senior managers report to him directly.

Meanwhile, Logitech's senior managers were clearly signaling that they welcomed speculative ventures that could be moonshots returning 1000 percent on investments. In late 2019, Logitech unveiled a new V.R. stylus, called the Logitech VR Ink Pilot Edition. The stylus is designed to allow people working with V.R. headsets to draw and sculpt shapes in virtual reality. Improving on existing V.R. controllers from HTC and Samsung, the Pilot seamlessly moves between drawing in the air and sketching on a table or any flat surface. It's not clear what market the product will land in; the demo video shows a Pilot in use in computer-assisted design, implying a future as an expensive professional tool. The Pilot is a salvo into a V.R. market that is still maturing; if it fails, Logitech's product team will have garnered valuable experience in a field that may be the next consumer-technology bonanza.

Recognizing "People" People

One other practice of Darrell's that stands the company in good stead is staying in touch with his employees. Review after review on Glassdoor remarks on how he spends time with employees and listens to their points of view.

None of this should be taken as minimizing the company's struggles in making this transformation. There have been failed products. Reallocating the R&D money resulted in some anger and fear. Middle-level managers struggled to acclimate to the new environment. But the numbers bear Darrell out. Profits have more than quintupled; the company now derives less than 50 percent of its revenues from the sales of keyboards and mice, and it is now a perennial winner of prestigious design awards. Investors have likewise benefited. Share prices have risen by more than 450 percent since their nadir, when Darrell joined.

After five years as CEO, Darrell decided to undertake an exercise of firing himself and assessing whether he would hire himself back. It sounds like a gimmick, but Darrell was seriously considering whether he was the right guy for the job. He decided he was an acceptable candidate after all.

Case Study 2: From Evil Empire to Cool Kid: Microsoft's Stunning Cultural Transformation

Every person, organization, and even society reaches a point at which they owe it to themselves to hit refresh—to reenergize, renew, reframe, and rethink their purpose.

Satya Nadella, *Hit Refresh: The Quest to Rediscover Microsoft's Soul and Imagine a Better Future for Everyone*

When Satya Nadella was named the CEO of Microsoft Corporation, in February 2014, one of his first acts was to ask all the top executives at the famously combative software company to read Marshall Rosenberg's *Nonviolent Communication,* a book about how to communicate and collaborate effectively using compassion and understanding rather than competition and judgment.[2]

With that request, Nadella signaled to the company's leaders that he wanted to make a big change in the culture of the world's largest software company. Bill Gates, the company's longtime CEO, had been known for berating employees. Steve Ballmer, who succeeded Gates, made cringe-worthy YouTube bait with his on-stage screaming and sweaty-faced antics at company product launches. Both endorsed hardball business tactics that competitors feared and admired but customers loathed.

Nadella was cut from a different cloth. Calm, and described by some as beatific, Nadella was born in India and has an enduring love of cricket. He also embraces Buddhist beliefs and has long enjoyed a reputation for calm responses even in the most contentious circumstances and for focusing on positive feedback to reinforce good habits.

Move Fast, Fix Things, Be Nicer

From his first day on the job, Satya Nadella believed that things needed to change, and to change quickly. Microsoft was fading away. It had lost the battle for smartphones. Its primary revenue stream, from software licenses, was perceived as vulnerable as businesses moved away from desktop and server licenses and embraced cloud computing. Linux, the open-source operating system, was set to overtake Windows as the most widely used server operating system. In cloud computing, Amazon was well ahead of both Google Cloud and Microsoft's fledgling Windows Azure cloud service. Because the desktop-and server-license business lines controlled so much revenue, the company struggled to move talent to much smaller but faster-growing business lines. And the powerful Windows unit internally moved to quash any attempts to usurp its power.

As a result, Microsoft was in big trouble, even if it remained insanely profitable. Ballmer had tripled revenues and doubled profits, but Microsoft's stock price remained largely flat, a clear signal that investor perception was of a future not all that bright. At its core, this was a problem of lack of innovation, of a company trapped by its reliance on a revenue stream that, though enticing, was sure to fade, coming from a legacy product that was on the wrong side of history.

Nadella recognized this and moved swiftly. A former engineer from Sun Microsystems (a company recognized as a prolific producer of software visionaries), after joining Microsoft in 1992, Nadella had spent time in sales and other management functions and somehow managed to survive and thrive despite a mellow disposition, eventually becoming the executive running the nascent cloud business. As the new C.E.O., he knew that, in order to safeguard the company's future, he needed to set an entirely new tone for it and revamp its culture to make space for innovation and allow new initiatives to grow and succeed. He believed that central to this would be building empathy—a quality not previously associated with Microsoft.

Nadella made changes both small and large, both symbolic and immediately consequential. In his first public appearance after being named CEO, Nadella said that his company was all about mobile and cloud computing, two fields that were growing very quickly but in which Microsoft was playing second fiddle. He rushed to release the Office productivity suite for iPhones, a move that Microsoft executives had previously blocked out of fear that they would be helping rival Apple and undermining a key motivation for business users to purchase the failing Windows Phones.

More subtly, Nadella began removing the word *Windows* from conversations. He stopped referring to Microsoft's cloud as "Windows

Azure," signaling that Azure had its own important product line, distinct from the Windows unit. Then, in late March of 2014, he moved to remove Windows from the cloud product line's name, making his intentions even clearer. The future of Microsoft did not lie in trying to prop up the Windows dynasty for as long as possible.

Changing Culture

As a manager and a leader, too, Nadella made it clear that the old, aggressive behaviors were no longer welcome. Never raising his voice or showing overt anger at employees or executives, Nadella constantly worked to create a more comfortable environment. He never wrote angry emails, and he refused to tolerate anger or yelling in executive meetings. At the same time, he promoted a culture of curiosity and learning. He urged the company's 120,000+ employees to embrace a "learn-it-all" curiosity, in contrast to what he categorized as Microsoft's traditional "know-it-all" worldview. In the marathon Friday executive-team meetings, Nadella instituted a regular feature wherein Microsoft researchers would phone in to talk about their innovations—reminding the company's leaders of the company's advances and encouraging them to focus on the future rather than maintain the status quo.

In a break from the past, Microsoft no longer publicly touts hated enemies or bugaboos. Tensions remain, naturally: Microsoft regularly clashes with Amazon over matters of the cloud, and Nadella has gently prodded potential customers with the reminder that Amazon may one day try to eat their lunch. For the most part, though, Nadella has focused on burnishing the company's battered reputation. He has warmly embraced the open-source software community, giving Microsoft a credibility boost among developers, and has shown a willingness to partner with competitors, under the right circumstances. He has struck deals with Salesforce (which competes with Microsoft's CRM products) and Linux reseller Red Hat (which competes with

Microsoft's Windows Server division) to encourage them and their customers to use Microsoft's Azure cloud.

More importantly, Nadella has laid out a bold strategy and made bold moves. To begin with, he wrote off the entire Nokia acquisition and halted Microsoft's smartphone efforts in acknowledgment that it was a lost cause. In 2016, he oversaw the purchase of LinkedIn, the social media network for business executives, and, in 2018, GitHub, the social coding network housing the greatest proportion of the world's software projects. These are of a pattern: focusing on the future and revenue streams that are complementary to a vision of collaboration and selling cloud-based products and services. Those two purchases contrast with the Nokia purchase, a seemingly desperate attempt to salvage a mobile hardware future and a vision of Windows dominance that did not conform with reality. (Incidentally, both GitHub and LinkedIn are worth considerably more today than what Nadella paid for them.)

Nadella's clearest and most consequential move, though, came in March 2018, roughly four years after he took over as CEO. In an email to all employees titled "Embracing Our Future: Intelligent Cloud and Intelligent Edge," Nadella announced that he would split the old Windows Development Group into two separate engineering groups, one called "Experiences and Devices" and the other called "Cloud + A.I. Platform." This move cemented the company's commitment to moving away from Windows and putting the bulk of resources into projects fueling innovation rather than stagnation. It was a bold move and one that met with much grumbling from insiders and people on the old Windows teams. But Nadella was certain that this was Microsoft's best path. In reality, it was the final big step in Nadella's plan to reorient the company: it left him, and the rest of Microsoft, free to face the future.

The results of Nadella's efforts have been nothing short of spectacular. The company's market capitalization has nearly quintupled, from roughly $300 billion at Nadella's ascension to more than $1.4

trillion as of early 2020, and Microsoft has become the most valuable company in the world, surpassing Apple and Google. Contributing to this market validation are several successes. First, Microsoft has been wildly successful in converting desktop Office and Windows licenses to subscriptions to the Office365 suite of online productivity products, swapping its lucrative license model for an even more lucrative and stable Software-as-a-Service (SaaS) business model.

Next, Microsoft Azure, now in second place to Amazon's cloud properties, is making steady headway against them, and is enjoying strong growth in sales of a host of more lucrative SaaS offerings, including its CRM and business analytics platforms.

Even the Microsoft Surface tablet has emerged as a quiet market success, taking some of the dominant iPad's market share.

Finally, amidst all this, sales of Windows operating systems on PCs and of Windows Server continue to grow slowly and remain highly profitable; so pulling revenues away from legacy products with slow development timelines may turn out not to have hurt their sales much after all.

What enabled these dramatic changes was the new culture of humility, acceptance of change, and openness to external ideas. The resulting successes bear out Nadella's *Hit Refresh* claim "Culture eats strategy for breakfast," and Microsoft's reinvention has clearly sown the seeds of further success.

Case Study 3: Riding the Exponential Curve: NextEra Energy Demonstrates Innovation in a Utility

If it were a country, NextEra Energy, a Florida-based utility, would rank seventh in the world in wind-energy generation. The company is the largest private generator of wind energy on the planet today, with dozens of windfarms dotting the landscapes of Texas, the United States'

Great Plains, and the Pacific Northwest. From humble beginnings as a small local utility in Florida, NextEra Energy became an early pioneer in renewables. It has grown to become the world's largest electric-utility company by market capitalization. (Disclosure: Vivek has been an occasional adviser to the firm and run a masterclass on exponential innovation with its executives.)

A Toe in the Water

What NextEra Energy perceived and acted on that others did not was the exponential curve of renewable technologies' progress. The company did exactly as we are advocating in this book: understand the advances in and convergences of technologies and invest accordingly. NextEra's managers wagered in the early 2000s that the costs of solar- and wind-energy generation would fall dramatically even as the costs of traditional energy sources remained steady or rose. That looked like an enormous opportunity to expand the company's reach and profits just ahead of the rest of the energy industry. The gamble paid off in spectacular fashion as demand for wind and solar energy took off and prices, as predicted, plummeted.

NextEra's managers called this its "toe in the water" strategy: an effort to invest in a variety of energy-related areas in order to test its ideas and capabilities. Other areas into which NextEra has expanded include power-transmission cables, battery farms and other installations for storage of renewable energy, and natural-gas pipelines. In all these areas, NextEra has expanded greatly over the past six years.

NextEra took these steps because it foresaw what the energy future would look like and the competitive competencies the company would require. It consistently identified key trends well ahead of market forces. For example, it correctly predicted that shareholder activism would increase demand for renewables in 2017. It also realized that coal plants would come offline sooner than anyone realized and that demand for coal was in steep decline, opening up even more opportunities for renewables. Following the exponential curve of renewable price declines, NextEra correctly predicted that the volume of solar and wind development in the United States would exceed forecasts—as it did, by a factor of five to ten. "The pace of wind and solar development have been consistently underestimated," company CEO Jim Robo said in his June 2019 investor presentation.

Talent, Consistency, and Foresight

Jim Robo is only the company's third CEO since 1989. He joined in 2002 as vice president of corporate development and strategy before leading the company's competitive business and then serving as chief operating officer. Robo came to NextEra Energy after nearly a decade in leadership roles at General Electric. He was, he says, fortunate to have worked for seven people who were—or became—CEOs of Fortune 500 companies, from the legendary Jack Welch to his own immediate predecessor as CEO of NextEra Energy, Lew Hay.

Robo describes a CEO's main three responsibilities as capital allocation, execution, and talent development. The importance of capital allocation in the electric utility industry is clear; indeed, NextEra Energy is one of the top five U.S. capital investors in any industry. Yet Robo reminds investors that what distinguishes one company from the next is the consistency of their execution and the quality of their talent. On execution, although Robo freely admits that NextEra Energy has made its share of $10 million mistakes, he says that it is thanks to superior execution that the company has avoided the billion-dollar write-offs of many of its peers. As for talent, it's a topic that investors may raise less than they should, but it's what Robo credits as a key competitive advantage for NextEra Energy.

The company was also a pioneer in using machine learning and big data to improve maintenance and utility-grid reliability. It began installing smart meters and microgrids to better manage demand in the early 2010s, well before the 2018 and 2019 California wildfires and subsequent outages made better demand management a matter of necessity for all utilities. In a similar vein, NextEra is among the leaders in applying machine learning to utility problems. These can predict problems in the grid and in generation locations—even remote ones, where wind farms are located.

The company deploys a large fleet of drones equipped with advanced cameras and machine-vision software to monitor its facilities for pending problems. All these technologies have led to increases in reliability and significantly reduced outages.

NextEra has also embraced other forward-thinking innovation practices we have outlined in this book. In an annual contest for employee-generated ideas that it calls Project Accelerate, for example, from 2013 to 2019, the company received submissions of 18,000 ideas. It evaluated 11,000 of them, and 5,600 were deemed good enough to merit further exploration. Some of the ideas that NextEra put into practice included improving work processes, automating various data-entry functions, and insourcing certain job functions.

The company consistently cites these contests and participation as the main reason for its ability to report the best operations and maintenance numbers in the entire United States for utilities. Better still, by including employees in the ideation and innovation process, the company has kept its workforce engaged and learning. Turnover is low, and promotion from within is how the company predominantly fills its management ranks.

The company's shareholders have benefited in a big way: the price of NextEra issues has increased roughly six-fold in the decade since 2010, not including dividend increases. Clearly it pays to dip your toe in the water, try new things, teach your employees—and ride the exponential curves.

Case Study 4: How Tech Mahindra Leaps Forward by Eating its Own Dogfood

In May 2020, with the coronavirus rampaging through India and the world, C.P. Gurnani was struggling with a problem that all bosses faced: how to keep his workers safe. As C.E.O. of the Indian technology giant Tech Mahindra, Gurnani had to care for a global workforce of 125,000, of whom a third were in India. This was critical not only for their welfare but also for sustaining the operations of the thousand global companies whose systems they manage.

The first step, Gurnani knew, was to make it easy for his workers to know their present health status and their risks upon exposure to the coronavirus. Legacy testing systems were not an option: labs everywhere were overwhelmed, and reagents and protective gear were in short supply. As well, he did not want his employees to have to stand in line with possibly sick people and thereby acquire infection.

Rather than rely on old names in health care, Gurnani turned to HealthCubed, a startup with its roots in India that was attacking the problem in a very innovative way. The company was originally founded to make it easy for the poor in India to gain access to rapid and affordable medical testing for hundreds of common ailments and conditions. A hardware platform with artificial intelligence-based software and an array of sensors, the product—HealthCube—was designed as a consumer device with medical-grade capabilities and had been used on more than a million patients in India and Africa. (Full disclosure: Vivek is an advisor to and investor in HealthCubed.)

Gurnani could see how a technology designed for the poor could be repurposed for corporate use, and he understood the benefits it would provide. A full range of tests, including tests for blood pressure, oxygen saturation, blood glucose, hemoglobin and cholesterol, and antibody tests for COVID-19 would cost less than Rs. 1,000 per employee. And more importantly, they would enable every employee to be tested frequently and receive instant results on their smartphones that they could have a high degree of confidence in. The tests could be administered in the offices by nurses or physician assistants, or even by office managers with a few hours of training.

HealthCubed's foray into COVID-19 diagnostics began with a call by Gurnani to its C.E.O., Ramanan Laxminarayan, asking what it would take for him to add SARS-CoV-2 antigen and antibody tests to the product and then commanding that he step on the gas and get it done as soon as possible.

Gurnani knew that if the technology allowed his company to operate in safety, it could do so for all his customer businesses, too. This is also an extension of Tech Mahindra's push to become among the best workplaces in India—and the entire world. Gurnani recognized that talent today is global and it moves where it wants to. By creating a working environment that helps employees be their best selves, respects and values their families and prioritizes making their jobs more rewarding, Tech Mahinda is better able to attract and retain the talent that is the least common denominator for sustaining an innovation culture.

The Reinvention of Tech Mahindra

The adoption of HealthCube for COVID-19 testing in Tech Mahindra was emblematic of how this company, with roots in the original Indian I.T. revolution, has become a modern tech innovator—and of how quickly it can make decisions to take on bold, original solutions to challenging problems. In fact, the company has evolved into something completely different than its origins.

In the early 2000s, while at Duke University's Pratt School of Engineering, Vivek researched the rapid rise of I.T. services and outsourcing firms in India. These companies, with the advantages of a well-educated, English-speaking workforce, rapidly became the back office for many global businesses. But around 2010, their fortunes began to fall. Many of the core businesses they had built using call centres, low-level I.T. management, and accounting were now facing threats from two directions: even cheaper outsourcing and I.T. services firms in China and Vietnam, and advancing technologies that were replacing the foundations of entire industries. Vivek noted that these I.T. companies had become complacent, constantly patting themselves on the back and revelling in their past successes.

Multinational customers regularly played Indian firms off against one another in contract-bidding wars. And none of these firms was willing to take the risks inherent in entering new industries such as health care or even in innovating to provide added value. Such reluctance left them unable to develop in-house products or customize software to meet global standards that produced high incomes for the larger tech consultancies, such as IBM and Accenture. Employees too had become technologically complacent, receiving continual wage increases merely by job-hopping.

As this played out in the decade after 2010, Vivek turned pessimistic on the Indian I.T. miracle and warned the industry's executives that they would go the way of the dinosaurs unless they urgently reinvented themselves. Part of his reasoning was that many of the offerings of Indian firms were in danger of antiquation through automation. Back-office tech services, he believed, were going to become the shoe factories of the technology sector: low margin, lower skilled, and less economically dynamic.

Vivek was not alone in noticing this troubling trend. After growing up in the small town of Neemuch in Rajasthan, India, C.P. Gurnani had worked his way up the ladder at an array of Indian and U.S. outsourcing firms that did business in the subcontinent. He had earned a reputation for smart leadership at Tech Mahindra through the challenging acquisition and turnaround of a scandal-ridden I.T.-services firm, Satyam. This acquisition turned into a multi-year odyssey that led Gurnani to consider what India's technology industry would have to become in order to remain relevant into the 21st century.

Gurnani had watched as tech giants in the United States took off and Amazon, Apple, Salesforce, and Google completely reshaped how developers, marketers, executives, consumers, and almost everyone else thought about tech. In this environment of rapid change, he recognized that I.T.-service firms have to embrace the principles that have made those iconic companies successful. Specifically, this meant that Tech Mahindra, of which Gurnani became the managing director in 2014, would need to emulate those U.S. leaders in thinking more as a startup and less as a tech giant.

Gurnani recognized that setting appropriate expectations and inculcating new modes of thought and action in his workers would necessitate codifying the guiding principles in a set of values and programs. To this end, Tech Mahindra created an industry-agnostic platform for service delivery, which it called New Age Delivery, to foster both internal innovation and improvement in external delivery of products and services to customers. Behind this novel platform were some core ideas:

- Shift from reacting to learning and adapting rapidly.
- Be frugal and re-use rather than reinvent—user stories as well as code.
- Use internal and external marketplaces' self-service capabilities of enabling customers to rate, curate, and access resources (such as people and intellectual property).
- Embrace the use of the most advanced analytics, automation, and A.I. capabilities to improve efficiency and quality as well as learn and adapt.
- Transform the Tech Mahindra workforce by such engaging methods as gamification, social proof, and user-experience design.

- As Amazon did, make the platform ready to create a range of services via application-programming interfaces.

The larger goal was to make Tech Mahindra's services independent of other people's technology by creating customized offerings ready for transformation into products and re-use by the broader market—and, above all, to centre its processes on its customers, listening to them very closely before partnering with them on a solution. This was a shift that pushed Tech Mahindra up the value chain and into the risky but rewarding terrain of creating a lot more original intellectual property—in making software, user experiences, and other technology realms.

Staying Relevant, Staying Nimble, and Building Acumos

Of course, Gurnani realized that changing the course of the company required more than the right words. So he crowdsourced ideas by asking his executives and employees how the company could stay at the forefront of change in an industry whose changes are accelerating.

The understanding that emerged was that the necessary changes could not be imposed from the top down and couldn't occur entirely within the walls of Tech Mahindra but should involve partners. A classic example is the Acumos Project, one of the world's leading A.I. efforts, housed inside the Linux Foundation. Acumos neatly encapsulates nearly all of Tech Mahindra's new foci, including curated marketplaces; A.I. and analytics; working with external partners in academia, and with customers; community and open-source efforts; and crowdsourcing innovation.

Tech Mahindra had worked closely with telecom giant AT&T to build Acumos as a next-generation A.I. platform that could become an open-source commons and marketplace for technology useful in developing A.I. The goal of Acumos was to create the equivalent of the

Linux operating system in A.I. development: an open-source platform to which researchers and programmers could easily add the most useful existing technology, such as Google's TensorFlow, in a form easy to base applications upon. To that end, Acumos was designed as a basis for any type of A.I.-as-a-Service applications and to make those applications accessible via standardized application-programming interfaces.

Tech Mahindra wrote the code for the marketplace and, to let it run inside Acumos, incorporated data-processing elements in common use in A.I. applications, creating the A.I. equivalent of Amazon Web Services. Unlike Amazon Web Services, though, Acumos is community owned and operated, no considerations of profit compromising participation and development. Federated in nature, Acumos can run as a public, private, or gated community platform, and Acumos packages that run on one Acumos node are readily useable on others.

In this way, technology developed by Tech Mahindra for A.I. can be "dogfooded" internally before it is either offered to customers or pushed out into the open-source realm.

Eating your own dogfood is a technique that Gurnani uses to force his employees to stay ahead of the curve and provide great value to customers. Before offering back-to-work services to customers, Gurnani had his own workers use the HealthCube technology. And before asking employees to be tested with this, he had it used on himself, his family, and household workers.

In joining efforts such as Acumos, Tech Mahindra has been able to recruit talented workers by empowering them to work on intrinsically interesting technology projects. He knows that smart technologists will go where the interesting problems are. This is why, for example, Tech Mahindra has a team researching quantum computing, one of the hottest areas on the cutting edge of computational research. The company has moved to embrace risk and open up new frontiers aggressively.

Reinventing Tech Mahindra for the Long Haul

For Gurnani, the ultimate goal is not an improvement in the balance sheet but a long-term cultural transformation that will play out over decades—the kind of transformation that Satya Nadella's reinvention of Microsoft's culture accomplished. By applying modern innovation methodologies to cutting-edge technology and trends, Gurnani is imbuing Tech Mahindra with an innovation ethos that will outlast his tenure and alter the firm's image in the minds of its employees, its customers, and the world.

In that sense, innovation can become a self-perpetuating cycle. An organization such as Tech Mahindra, once it learns what it feels like to move at light speed, innovate, make rapid decisions, and embrace change, tends to find that—as when a building replaces a fast Internet connection with a slow WiFi one—the way they work and move and think changes to become faster, more nimble, more connected and more closely aligned with each other and with customers.

And that is a hallmark of innovation: the ability, even the necessity, to take risks, move fast, learn, fail, and succeed at an ever-increasing rate.

15

Innovation Management in Government

CHAPTER SUMMARY: Governments can contribute significantly to economic activity. This chapter looks at fostering innovation in government, the requirements for engendering success in government innovation programs, and how government innovation-management structures differ from the private sector's. We also look at the five requisites of government innovation and explain why we think we are in the midst of a golden age of government technological innovation.

The most famous government unit in the United Kingdom is probably the intelligence agency that the James Bond movies call MI6. In policy circles, though, it is the Behavioural Insights Team, known informally as the "nudge unit," that gets the attention.[1] Established in 2010 under Prime Minister David Cameron, the unit was named after the book *Nudge,* written by Nobel Prize-winning economist Richard Thaler and Holberg Prize winner Cass Sunstein.[2] *Nudge* discussed how government and businesses could significantly improve outcomes through small changes to human behavior that Thaler called nudges.

For example, Thaler highlighted research that showed that if retirement savings were switched from an opt-in to an opt-out setting, workers would save more money. Research by the U.S. retirement giant Vanguard, which administers millions of workers' retirement plans, documented that firms with opt-in retirement-plan enrollment enjoyed only 59 percent employee participation. In contrast, companies with automatic enrollment had an 86 percent participation rate.

The nudge unit was controversial at first. Critics derided the team of academics, economists, and psychologists as disconnected from reality. But the nudge team racked up considerable successes through small changes. For example, it suggested making a small change to tax-collection notices, stating the percentage of people who paid their taxes on time. This simple tactic yielded real improvements in the speed and rate of tax payments in an experiment on 200,000 real taxpayers.[3] So the British government adopted the tactic.

In another experiment, the nudge unit worked with four government agencies to increase organ donation by testing eight different messages requesting that people join the organ donation registry. It tested these in a randomized fashion on roughly a million visitors, becoming one of the largest social science experiments in history. The winning message appealed to empathy, saying: "If you needed an organ transplant, would you have one? If so, please help others." It is estimated that this experiment added more than 100,000 organ donors to the registry.[4]

The nudge unit was deemed successful enough to spin out as a "social purpose company," jointly owned by its employees, the Cabinet Office, and an innovation charity, Nesta.[5] With dozens if not hundreds of policy successes to its credit, it now works with governments all over the world and is an oft-cited example of government innovation that works. It was part of a wave of experimentation attempted in the United Kingdom in the decade from 2010. This experimentation was in part due to extended austerity and reductions in government spending but was also motivated by the defining mantra of the longstanding conservative government: do more with less.

Moving People's Cheese Is Harder When It's Government Cheese

Innovation management in government is harder than in business but often more valuable. It is usually more complicated too, because of rules, regulations, and political considerations. Nearly all government innovation must happen entirely in public view, rendering it susceptible to derailment by aggressive political constituencies even if it is certain to yield improvements. Even the barest hint of corruption can shut down a project that has tremendous promise, and missteps are far more likely to become public debacles, painful for government leaders and workers alike.

Internal adoption of innovation can be hamstrung by internal rules and regulations designed to ensure fairness or transparency that, though they may do precisely that, also slow its implementation.

Real changes to incumbent structures often threaten jobs if they are to deliver fiscal "efficiency," resulting in resistance from workers and their unions. Taxpayers themselves are fickle adopters of new technology efforts; if a product in the consumer realm must be ten times easier, then one in the government realm should be fifteen times easier. And taxpayer criticism can quickly scuttle or delay innovation efforts in the field, reducing the necessary adoption period and innovations' endurance.

Perhaps most insidious of all, all too often, extraordinary performance that reduces costs results in reducing resources to the department that logged the success; concurrently, overuse or misuse of resources is encouraged by the "use-it-or-lose-it" reality of most government agency funding cycles and policies.

That said, government innovation can be done. Done well, it can have tremendous impact. In New York City, for example, former Mayor

Michael Bloomberg and his team conceived of and instituted a novel phone-based system that functions like a city concierge and analyzes calls to prioritize maintenance and policing. Bloomberg also installed a culture of data-based management and systems to monitor New York City in a way previously unimaginable. This data focus led to a decade of astounding improvements in the provision of city services and helped improve the quality of life in a city once deemed unmanageable.

We will explore several other examples of innovation management in cities and governments. Fortunately, many of the tactics applicable to the private sector work well in the public sector too. Innovation prizes to solicit proposals to solve public and government problems are a proven recipe, and, in a similar vein, crowdsourcing of ideas from broad swathes of the electorate has been shown to yield promising results.

One apparently common aspect is government innovation's greater dependence on external expertise, particularly with regard to technology. Government bodies are generally not equipped for innovative technology development. Rarely are they scholars of user experience, and they are not generally accustomed to testing new products on customers.

Fortunately, governments are more open now than ever before to innovation partnerships. Throughout the developed world, government organizations realize the need to make good use of technology if they are to effect change. In the United Kingdom and the United States in particular, conditions of constant austerity have forced consideration of changes that previously might have been unimaginable. India went as far as rechristening its planning and policy ministry the National Institution for Transforming India (also called NITI Aayog) so that it could focus on instituting innovation in its federal and state governments. The reality is that governments must do more with less. Here are some ways in which they can.

Five Requisites for Government Innovation

Over the course of 2014, Clayton Christensen and two other researchers from the Harvard Business School interviewed public-sector innovators, surveyed hundreds of government initiatives, and held a conference on the topic at the school in order to gather information and bring together the community. Christensen's team identified five core requisites for public-sector innovation:[6]

- Ability to experiment
- Ability to replace outdated infrastructure
- Existence of feedback loops
- Existence of incentives for product or service improvement
- Existence of budget constraints on end users

Christensen's team analyzed how the District of Columbia (Washington, DC) had managed to move from coin-operated parking meters to a system of using mobile-phone apps to pay for parking spaces. Parking is a major problem in many cities: people driving into cities may spend 20 percent to 30 percent of their driving time searching for parking, contributing significantly to gridlock and to carbon emissions; simply paying parking meters can entail difficulties; and a shopper needing extra time has to run back to the car to top up the meter.

The phone-app system offered drivers with smartphones very clear benefits from the beginning. The city would no longer need to pay coin collectors to drive around the city to gather all the coins. This enabled workers to spend their time on more valuable tasks; it also lowered carbon emissions and was less hassle for those who could pay by tapping on an app rather than digging around in seat cushions or carrying coins in their bags and wallets.

The city engaged a third party to build an app called ParkMobile that was to replace the parking meters. With careful change management, consultation with public-sector unions, and some user testing, ParkMobile ended up a major success within two years of its October 2012 launch. There were bumps in the road: on occasion, fines resulted from late information updates to meter readers. The fees per transaction made parking for shorter periods pricier than it had been. And, in its early versions, users had to input their license-plate details and the correct parking zone, a process that resulted in many manual errors.

The switch to a mobile payment platform nonetheless unlocked many benefits. Washington, DC, began to use "demand-based" pricing, raising or lowering meter costs according to usage in an area.

Also, by switching meters from mechanical to electronic platforms, the city could remotely upgrade units and change pricing and terms. Today, ParkMobile is used by cities all over the United States, including seven of the ten largest metropolitan areas, and even for public parking lots that do not have meters. ParkMobile was so successful that the German automaker BMW purchased the company in 2018 as part of its effort to better understand transit solutions.

Of the innovation requirements laid out above, the ParkMobile installation clearly fits all five. The city government had the ability to experiment and was willing and able to replace outdated infrastructure. There were feedback loops in place; consumers are very vocal about their experiences, with consistent media coverage of ParkMobile problems. The city had a strong incentive to improve its service delivery—parking services—both to save money and to improve the user experience. The end user had real budget constraints. The perennially strapped city certainly could not endure cost overruns. The consumers were unwilling to pay high prices for parking spots; they would have voted with their feet and parked in private lots or ridden on public transit instead.

This is a high-cost example of innovation that requires years of planning. In general, the lower the capital expenditure required for a government innovation, the easier the implementation. The economically challenged city of Milwaukee, Wisconsin, is experimenting with placing mini-libraries in laundromats. The theory is that women (and it is mostly women, unfortunately) in poor neighborhoods must wash clothes and watch their children simultaneously.[7] So the hope is that, given the opportunity, these mothers will spend that time reading with their little ones; a large body of research has demonstrated that young children strongly benefit from being read to. The libraries will also allow book borrowing, enabling children to read at home. This is another easy public-education hack: studies have associated children's performance in school with the number of books in their homes.

Such an innovation is comparatively low cost and easy to test the effect of via a small number of laundromats. Government innovation can also be nearly zero cost, when the government works with another party to provide a benefit that is free but valuable. In Monongalia County in Pennsylvania, the county health department faced a rise in the number of syphilis cases. The department used its existing marketing channels but also tried a new one to reach a wide audience: dating apps. The county asked a popular dating app maker to post syphilis warnings when users from the county logged into the app.[8] This raised awareness and contributed to public health efforts. It cost the county nothing but achieved a wide reach nearly immediately. Thus, exponentially advancing technology can also provide, for free and to a limitless constituency, benefits that otherwise would cost real money or effort to pull together.

A Golden Age of Government Technological Innovation

Despite the political turmoil evident all over the world, we just may be sustaining a golden age of government innovation. The factors that have facilitated effective innovation in the private sector carry the same weight in most cases of technological innovation in the public sector. Just as we benefit from getting free GPS information via our smartphones, so can we benefit by paying for parking meters or other government services via apps, remotely and without needing legal tender or wasting time to top up our meters.

Moreover, real government expenditure has never undone the broad government budget cuts due to the 2008 economic crash. The pressure to do more with less is acute. Necessity has always been the mother of invention, as the saying goes, but in the case of the United Kingdom as a nation, and many states of the United States, austerity is now deeply ingrained in the government ethos and is unlikely to reverse for years to come.

So the options are few. One of the best of them is innovation through technology. More global citizens are connected to the Internet via powerful smartphones than ever before. Those phones are enabling huge leaps in government innovation. Cheap sensors have rendered environmental data easy to collect. Smartphones and other technology are empowering citizen participation in government innovation to degrees not previously contemplated, enabling rapid feedback and faster decision-making. Cities and countries are turning to analysis of large datasets in order to understand where opportunities for improvement lie. These same environmental data-collecting and data-sharing capabilities can also help factories produce higher-quality goods. Ambient temperature and humidity can dramatically affect manufacturing processes; monitoring and understanding these effects will contribute substantially to the ability of Industry 4.0 to deliver on the promise of making more, higher-quality goods with the same physical plant.

As they are everywhere else, exponential changes in technology in the civic realm will only accelerate, increasing and improving opportunities to remake government through innovation thinking, humane design principles, and the other keys to rapid innovation in the private sector.

CONCLUSION

You Can't Ignore It; How Can You Embrace It?

In April 2019, Sainsbury's opened its first cash-free store in Holborn Circus, London. It was the first of its kind in the United Kingdom, ahead of other grocers and their nemesis, Amazon.com. At the tech-heavy convenience store, shoppers can scan the items they wish to buy with their phones, drop them into a cart, and be charged on the way out, no human attendants or cash registers required. Sainsbury's stated goal was to provide a more seamless shopping experience; but the real motivation for the rollout may have had something to do with all the publicity that Amazon was receiving for its Amazon Go stores. In these stores, shoppers don't even need to scan an item; they just need to have the Amazon Go app on their phones open. They can select what they want, drop it into their cart, and just walk out. Sainsbury's store is not quite that smooth, but the speed with which Sainsbury's managed to compete with Amazon was nonetheless impressive.

This kind of responsiveness will be essential for organizations' survival into the future. Technology is evolving in surprising bursts and becoming ever more affordable. Advances in A.I., computing, networks, and sensors are making possible trillion-dollar industries—and the destruction of legacy ones over a matter of years. Technology that formerly only the rich had access to is now available to everyone, everywhere. Most of the world is now connected to the Internet, increasingly with very fast broadband connections. As the world's entrepreneurs learn from one another, they will increasingly discover responses to large problems both in their own backyards and for people living thousands of miles away, and humanity will benefit from this sea change.

Legacy businesses, however, will need to update their playbooks. As we discussed earlier in this book, the models of innovation and disruption captured in Clayton Christensen's *The Innovator's Dilemma,* once a guiding light on how to survive industry disruptions, are now outdated.

The old innovation texts teach companies to look in the wrong places for competitive threats and encourage them to separate the innovative disruptors from the core businesses and put them into new company divisions. In an era in which advancing technologies converge and allow industries to encroach on and disrupt one another, companies will need to embrace disruptive technologies and have all of their people working together to take on the new competitive threats.

Legacy organizations need to expand their view of what disruption is and where it may come from. For example, Christensen originally believed that Uber and Tesla Motors could not be genuinely disruptive because they did not match his definition of disruptive innovation, where disruptive competition enters the lower end or an unserved part of a market before floating upward into the mainstream market. Uber has gone in exactly the opposite direction, as Christensen said in a 2015 *Harvard Business Review* paper, "building a position in the mainstream market first and subsequently appealing to historically overlooked segments."[1]

As for Tesla, the electric car juggernaut that began by selling to the high end of the market, Christensen and his co-authors wrote: "If disruption theory is correct, Tesla's future holds either acquisition by a much larger incumbent or a years-long and hard-fought battle for market significance."[2]

Tesla's Model 3, a mid-priced sedan, is selling in far higher numbers than any other electric car today, as it moves down market in order to reach more customers. And Tesla has already grown too large to buy. Realistically, only three companies—Apple, Google, and Microsoft—have both the market capitalization and the cash to buy Tesla. Musk has effectively priced his company beyond the reach of any suitor in the car industry. Tesla is in fact more likely to acquire General Motors, Ford, and Volkswagen than to have to fend them off.

In upsetting the taxi industry, Uber came out of nowhere, and it too began from the top down. At first, Uber tried competing with high-end limousines. Then it launched UberX to offer cheap taxi service. Now it competes in food delivery, trucking and logistics, and other services. Uber is challenging supermarkets, a raft of food delivery startups, and FedEx—simultaneously. And it continues to try to build self-driving cars.

Apple, which has already disrupted the mobile-phone and music industries, now has its eye on health care and finance. The increasingly popular Apple Watch functions as a medical device, and Apple's ResearchKit is being used in hundreds of clinical trials. Apple Watches have, in several cases, notified a wearer of a potentially life-threatening heart condition called atrial fibrillation. In time, the Apple Watch will overturn the pharmaceutical industry by keeping track of the effectiveness and side effects of the drugs we take and helping us improve our lifestyle and habits so that we rely less on medication. For its part, Amazon is now offering a health application to its employees that includes video consultations and other ways to access health plans.

If history is a guide, we may expect this application—and full-blown health plans—to be in the offing from Amazon.

In the field of payment and finance, roughly 51 percent of all retail outlets in the United States now accept payment via Apple Pay, and adoption is increasing as people recognize its convenience. Apple is also edging into banking, opening a credit card with the help of the major investment bank Goldman Sachs. Oh, and Google is opening a business line offering customers savings and checking accounts. Facebook's CEO, Mark Zuckerberg, still wants to take on the global currency systems with his Libra cryptocurrency—despite all the opposition it faces from policymakers. And Goldman Sachs's personal savings unit, Marcus, provides no-fee personal loans and high-yield online savings for individuals, pushing the company squarely into the consumer market, into which it has said it never wanted to tread.

Moreover, Google, SpaceX, and Amazon are in a race to provide high-speed Internet access throughout the world via microsatellites and balloons. At first, they will boost the services of telecom companies; then they will eat their lunch. After all, if we have WiFi everywhere, why will we need to buy mobile data from the phone companies? Google has already entered the global wireless market with an affordable plan for its Google Fi service that treats the wireless networks run by the major providers as commodities by enabling Google subscribers to flip back and forth across multiple networks to obtain the best signal. It could provide Internet access for free—just as it does maps, search, and email facilities—in exchange for a peek at our data.

As you can see from the dizzying array of developments, exponential disruption is no longer a narrow field that can be handled by a new company division or department. Companies that were born in the exponential era are leveraging new technologies to quickly move into adjacent or even totally novel industries.

Disruption is beginning to break out wherever technology can be applied, and existing companies need all hands on deck—with all divisions working together to find ways to reinvent themselves and defend themselves from the onslaught of new competition. This companywide, sometimes industrywide, effort requires bold new thinking and a vastly accelerated pace of innovation. Companies that fail to embrace innovation culture and re-engineer their organizations for exponential technological advances will lag and wither, and the turnover in the Fortune 500 will continue to accelerate. On the near horizon lurk new waves of change: augmented and virtual reality, quantum computing, voice computing, delivery drones, personalized medicine, free energy, and more.

The good news is that any company can become an innovation company by making the right changes, embracing the newer tactics, and, most importantly, unleashing the power of its people to think more broadly, act more ambitiously, and dream more wildly. Legacy companies have many advantages, and the ones that make that focus a cornerstone of their culture will have a leg up, regardless of what they face.

NOTES

Preface

1. Hannah Boland, "Amazon Plans Cashierless Store at Heart of London's West End," *The Telegraph* (December 10, 2018), https://www.telegraph.co.uk/technology/2018/12/09/amazon-plans-cashierless-store-heart-londons-west-end.

2. Glenn Taylor, "Sainsbury's Pilots Cashierless Checkout Store," Retail Touchpoints (April 30, 2019), https://retailtouchpoints.com/topics/digital-marketing/mobile-marketing/sainsbury-s-pilots-cashierless-checkout-store.

3. Vivek Wadhwa and Alex Salkever, *The Driver in the Driverless Car: How Your Technology Choices Create the Future,* 2nd ed. (Oakland, California: Berrett-Koehler, 2019).

Introduction

4. Chris Gebhart, "Falcon Heavy Soars; SpaceX Lands Critical NASA Double Asteroid Redirect Launch," NASA Spaceflight.com (April 12, 2019), https://www.nasaspaceflight.com/2019/04/falcon-heavy-spacex-nasa-asteroid-redirect.

5. Eric Berger, "SpaceX Details Its Plans for Landing Three Falcon Heavy Boosters at Once," Ars Technica (January 12, 2018), https://

arstechnica.com/science /2017/01/spacex-details-its-plans-for-landing-three-falcon-heavy-boosters-at-once.

6. Peter B. de Selding, "SpaceX's Reusable Falcon 9: What Are the Real Cost Savings for Customers?" *SpaceNews* (April 15, 2016), https://spacenews.com/ spacexs-reusable-falcon-9-what-are-the-real-cost-savings-for-customers.

7. "Boeing Tests Augmented Reality in the Factory," Boeing (January 19, 2018), https://www.boeing.com/features/2018/01/augmented-reality-01-18.page.

8. Dan Koeppel, "The Best Men's Razors (for Any Face)," Wirecutter (July 10, 2019), https://thewirecutter.com/reviews/best-manual-razor.

9. All dollar amounts in this book without a currency specification refer to U.S. dollars.

10. Michael Dubin and Diana Ransom, "How Dollar Shave Club Rode a Viral Video to Sales Success," *Inc.* (July-August 2015), https://www.inc.com/magazine /201507/diana-ransom/how-youtube-crashed-our-website.html.

11. Scott Cook, "#37 Gillette," *Forbes* (May 22, 2019), https://www.forbes.com/ companies/gillette/#3733984c10a0.

12. John Mannes, "Unilever Buys Dollar Shave Club for Reported $1B Value," Techcrunch (July 20, 2016), https://techcrunch.com/2016/07/19/unilever-buys-dollar-shave-club-for-reported-1b-value.

PART I: Why Exponential Disruptions Are Happening More Quickly and More Often

1. U.S. Healthweather™ Map (updated 22 May 2020), https://healthweather.us/ ?mode=C.+Atypical.

Chapter One: The Technological Basis of Breakthrough Disruption

1. In November 2019, Uber lost its license to operate in London, after Transport for London identified "several breaches that placed passengers and their safety at risk." This illustrates that taking advantage of new sources of competitive advantage does not obviate the need for compliance with the basics of good

operating methods. Costas Pitas, " 'Unfit' Uber Loses London License over Safety Failures" Reuters *Technology News* (November 25, 2019), https://www.reuters.com/article/us-uber-britain/unfit-uber-loses-london-license-over-safety-failures-idUSKBN1XZ0VL. After a battle with transportation regulators, the ride-hailing firm was granted an 18-month license on September 28, 2020.

2. "Garmin Market Cap 2006-2019," Mactotrends.net, https://www.macrotrends .net/stocks/charts/GRMN/garmin/market-cap (accessed April 17, 2020).

3. Howard Smith, "Garmin Stock Clears $100: Does It Still Have Room to Run?" *The Motley Fool* (January 28, 2020), https://www.fool.com/investing/2020/01/28/ garmin-stock-clears-100-does-it-have-room-to-run.aspx.

4. Ajay Agrawal, Joshua Gans, and Avi Goldfarb, *Prediction Machines: The Simple Economics of Artificial Intelligence* (Harvard: Harvard Business Review, 2018).

5. National Human Genome Research Institute, "The Cost of Sequencing a Human Genome," Genome.gov (October 30, 2019), https://www.genome.gov/about-genomics/fact-sheets/Sequencing-Human-Genome-cost.

6. The behavior and manipulation of minute quantities of fluids in narrow spaces.

Chapter Two: The Unexpected Consequences of Advancing Technologies

1. Jackie Fenn, "Meet Jackie Fenn: Gartner Analyst, Hype Cycle Inventor and Novelist," Gartner Blog (August 19, 2019), https://blogs.gartner.com/careers/2019/08/19/meet-jackie-fenn-gartner-analyst-hype-cycle-inventor-novelist.

2. Everett Rogers, *Diffusion of Innovations,* 5th ed. (New York and London: Simon & Schuster, 2003).

3. Nathan Bomey, "Shareholders of *USA TODAY* Owner Gannett and New Media Investment Group Approve Merger," *USA TODAY* (November 14, 2019), https://www.usatoday.com/story/money/2019/11/14/gannett-new-media-investment-group-merger-vote-results/2578352001.

Chapter Three: The Old Innovator's Dilemma versus the New Innovator's Dilemma

1. Clayton M. Christensen, *The Innovator's Dilemma: When New Technologies Cause Great Firms to Fail* (Harvard: Harvard Business Review Press, 2016).

2. Todd Spangler, "Netflix Bandwidth Consumption Eclipsed by Web Media Streaming Applications," *Variety* (September 10, 2019), https://variety.com/2019/ digital/news/netflix-loses-title-top-downstream-bandwidth-application-1203330313.

3. Benjamin Mullin and Lillian Rizzo, "Altice U.S.A. Buys Streaming-Video Network Cheddar for $200 Million," *The Wall Street Journal* (February 16, 2020), https://www.wsj.com/articles/altice-usa-buys-streaming-video-network-cheddar-for-200-million-11556640120.

4. "Bloomberg to Take Over BusinessWeek," *NBC News* (October 13, 2009), http://www.nbcnews.com/id/33299108.

5. Michael Corkery, "Sears, the Original Everything Store, Files for Bankruptcy," *The New York Times* (October 14, 2018), https://www.nytimes.com/2018/10/14/ business/sears-bankruptcy-filing-chapter-11.html.

6. Spencer Soper, "More than 50% of Shoppers Turn First to Amazon in Product Search," *Bloomberg* (September 27, 2016), https://www.bloomberg.com/news/articles/2016-09-27/more-than-50-of-shoppers-turn-first-to-amazon-in-product-search.

7. Julie Creswell, "How Amazon Steers Shoppers to Its Own Products," *The New York Times* (June 23, 2018), https://www.nytimes.com/2018/06/23/business/amazon-the-brand-buster.html.

8. James Vincent and Chaim Gartenberg, "Here's Amazon's New Transforming Prime Air Delivery Drone," *The Verge* (June 5, 2019), https://www.theverge.com/2019/6/5/18654044/amazon-prime-air-delivery-drone-new-design-safety-transforming-flight-video.

9. Max Chafkin, "Warby Parker Sees the Future of Retail," *Fast Company* (February 17, 2015), https://www.fastcompany.com/3041334/warby-parker-sees-the-future-of-retail.

10. Stefanie Fogel, "Tesla Model S Breaks Acceleration Record with Ludicrous Mode," *Engadget* (February 7, 2017), https://www.engadget.com/2017/02/07/ tesla-model-s-ludicrous-acceleration-record.

11. Travis Hoium, "Tesla's Solar Business Hits Another Roadblock," *The Motley Fool* (March 11, 2020), https://www.fool.com/investing/2020/03/11/teslas-solar-business-is-falling-apart.aspx.

PART II:
Why Top-Down Innovation Efforts Usually Fail

1. William Langewiesche, "What Really Brought Down the Boeing 737 Max?" *The New York Times Magazine* (September 18, 2019, revised January 21, 2020), https://www.nytimes.com/2019/09/18/magazine/boeing-737-max-crashes.html.

2. Erik Brynjolfsson and Andrew McAfee, *The Second Machine Age: Work, Progress, and Prosperity in a Time of Brilliant Technologies* (New York: W.W. Norton, 2016).

Chapter Four:
False Assumptions, Broken Models, Wasted Effort

1. Stuart W. Leslie and Robert H. Kargon, "Selling Silicon Valley: Frederick Terman's Model for Regional Advantage," *The Business History Review* 1996 winter 70, no. 4 (winter 1996^435-72, https://www.jstor.org/stable/3117312.

2. Antonio Regalado, "In Innovation Quest, Regions Seek Critical Mass," *MIT Technology Review* 116, no. 3 (July-August 2013), https://www.technologyreview.com/s/516501/in-innovation-quest-regions-seek-critical-mass.

3. AnnaLee Saxenian, *Regional Advantage: Culture and Competition in Silicon Valley* (Cambridge: Harvard University Press, 1996).

4. Vivek Wadhwa, AnnaLee Saxenian, Ben A. Rissing, and G. Gereffi, *America's New Immigrant Entrepreneurs: Part I* (Chapel Hill, NC: Duke University, 2007), https://papers.ssrn.com/sol3/papers.cfm?abstract_id=990152.

5. Lance Whitney, "Google Closes $3.2 Billion Purchase of Nest," CNet (February 12, 2014), https://www.cnet.com/news/google-closes-3-2-billion-purchase-of-nest.

6. "Capgemini Consulting and Altimeter Global Report Reveals Leading Businesses Continue to Struggle with Innovation, with Traditional R&D Model 'Broken,'" Capgemini (July 23, 2015), https://www.capgemini.

com/news/capgemini-consulting-and-altimeter-global-report-reveals-leading-businesses-continue-to.

7. Marc Andreessen, "The PMARCA Guide Startups: Part 4: The Only Thing That Matters," Pmarchive (June 25, 2007), https://pmarchive.com/guide_to_start ups_part4.html.

Chapter Five: The Rules of the Game Have Changed in Critical Ways

1. John Zealley, Robert Wollan, and Joshua Bellin, "Marketers Need to Stop Focusing on Loyalty and Start Thinking about Relevance," *Harvard Business Review* (March 21, 2018), https://hbr.org/2018/03/marketers-need-to-stop-focusing-on-loyalty-and-start-thinking-about-relevance.

2. Paige Leskin, "Inside the Rise of TikTok, the Viral Video-Sharing App Whose Ties to China Are Raising Concerns in the U.S.," *Business Insider Australia* (July 7, 2019), https://www.businessinsider.com.au/tiktok-app-online-website-video-sharing-2019-7.

3. Nick Statt, "TikTok's Global Social Media Takeover Is Starting to Slow Down," *The Verge* (November 4, 2019), https://www.theverge.com/2019/n/4/20948731/tiktok-bytedance-china-social-media-growth-users-decline-first-time.

4. Clay Shirky, *Here Comes Everybody: The Power of Organizing without Organizations* (London and New York: Penguin, 2008).

5. Don Tapscott and Anthony D. Williams, *Wikinomics: How Mass Collaboration Changes Everything* (London and New York: Penguin, 2006).

6. *Kevin Kelly, "1,000 True Fans" in Timothy Ferriss, Tools of Titans: The Tactics, Routines, and Habits of Billionaires, Icons, and World-Class Performers* (Boston: Houghton Mifflin Harcourt, 2016).

7. Michelle He Yee Lee, "Billionaire Owner of SoulCycle, Miami Dolphins Faces Backlash over Trump Fundraiser," *The Washington Post* (August 8, 2019), https:// www.washingtonpost.com/politics/billionaire-owner-of-soulcycle-miami-dolphins-endures-backlash-over-trump-fundraiser/2019/08/07/ce816790-b936-11e9-b3b4-2bb69e8c4e39_story.html.

Chapter Six: What Has Not Changed

1. Rob von Behren and Jonathan Wall, "Coming Soon: Make Your Phone Your Wallet," Google Blog (May 26, 2011), https://googleblog.blogspot.com/2011/05/ coming-soon-make-your-phone-your-wallet.html.

2. "Apple Pay Overtakes Starbucks as Top Mobile Payment App in the U.S.," eMarketer (October 23, 2019), https://www.emarketer.com/content/apple-pay-overtakes-starbucks-as-top-mobile-payment-app-in-the-us.

3. Peter Cohan, "Zoom Scoops Customers from Cisco in $16 Billion Video Conferencing Market," *Forbes* (3 October 3, 2017), https://www.forbes.com/sites/petercohan/2017/10/03/zoom-scoops-customers-from-cisco-in-16-billion-video conferencing-market.

Chapter Seven: The Eight Deadly Sins That Disable Change Efforts

1. Charles A. O'Reilly III and Michael L. Tushman, *Lead and Disrupt: How to Solve the Innovator's Dilemma* (Stanford, California: Stanford University Press, 2016), https://www.gsb.stanford.edu/faculty-research/books/lead-disrupt-how-solve-innovators-dilemma.

2. Philip Beeching, "Why Did HMV Fail?" *The Guardian* (January 16, 2013), https://www.theguardian.com/commentisfree/2013/jan/15/why-did-hmv-fail.

3. O'Reilly and Tushman, *Lead and Disrupt.*

4. Chris Smith, "Nike FuelBand: The Rise and Fall of the Wearable That Started It All," Wareable (February 22, 2016), https://www.wareable.com/fitness-trackers/ not-so-happy-birthday-nike-fuelband-2351.

5. Kaomi Goetz, "How 3M Gave Everyone Days Off and Created an Innovation Dynamo," *Fast Company* (January 2, 2011), 6, https://www.fastcompany.com/1663137/how-3m-gave-everyone-days-off-and-created-an-innovation-dynamo.

6. Hayagreeva Rao, Robert Sutton, and Allen P. Webb, "Innovation Lessons from Pixar: An Interview with Oscar-Winning Director Brad Bird," *McKinsey Quarterly* (April 2008), https://www.mckinsey.com/business-

functions/strategy-and-corporate-finance/our-insights/innovation-lessons-from-pixar-an-interview-with-oscar-winning-director-brad-bird.

7. Ellen McGirt, "How Cisco's CEO John Chambers Is Turning the Tech Giant Socialist," *Fast Company* (December 1, 2008), https://www.fastcompany.com/1093654/how-ciscos-ceo-john-chambers-turning-tech-giant-socialist.

8. Martha Lagace, "Gerstner: Changing Culture at IBM—Lou Gerstner Discusses Changing the Culture at IBM," Harvard Business School Working Knowledge (December 9, 2002), https://hbswk.hbs.edu/archive/gerstner-changing-culture-at-ibm-lou-gerstner-discusses-changing-the-culture-at-ibm.

9. Simon London, "Microsoft's Next Act," *McKinsey Quarterly* (April 2018), https://www.mckinsey.com/industries/technology-media-and-telecommunications/ our-insights/microsofts-next-act.

Chapter Eight: "Don't Buy This Jacket": Subverting Retail Expectations

1. Patagonia, "Don't Buy This Jacket, Black Friday and *The New York Times*," Patagonia (November 25, 2011), https://www.patagonia.com/blog//2011/n/dont-buy-this-jacket-black-friday-and-the-new-york-times.

2. Jeff Beer, "How Patagonia Grows Every Time It Amplifies Its Social Mission," *Fast Company* (March-April 2018), https://www.fastcompany.com/40525452/how-patagonia-grows-every-time-it-amplifies-its-social-mission.

Chapter Nine: Platform Technologies and Marketplaces

1. Rob Fijneman, Karina Kuperus, and Jochem Pasman, *Unlocking the Value of the Platform Economy: Mastering the Good, the Bad and the Ugly* (Amsterdam: Transformation Forums, 2018), https://dutchitchannel.nl/612528/dutch-transformation-platform-economy-paper-kpmg.pdf.

2. Geoffrey G. Parker, Marshall W. Van Alstyne, and Sangeet Paul Choudary, *Platform Revolution: How Networked Markets Are Transforming the Economy and How to Make Them Work for You* (New York: W. W. Norton, 2016).

Chapter Ten: How to (Dis)organize for Innovation

1. Dave Gershgorn and Harlan Murphy, "The 10 Greatest Home Innovations of the Year," *Popular Science* (October 19, 2016), https://www.popsci.com/10-greatest-home-innovations-year.

2. Barry Jaruzelski, Robert Chwalik, and Brad Goehle, "What the Top Innovators Get Right," *Strategy+Business* 93 (winter 2018), https://www.strategy-business.com/feature/What-the-Top-Innovators-Get-Right.

Chapter Eleven: The Tactics of Innovative Companies

1. Gov.UK, Innovation Funding Service, "SBRI: Competition in Railway Platform Edge and End Technology," Funding Competition (December 2019), https://apply-for-innovation-funding.service.gov.uk/competition/511/overview.

2. "Stuck at Prom Scholarship Contest," duckbrand.com 2020 (n.d.), https://www .duckbrand.com/stuck-at-prom.

3. "What Is Design Thinking?" IDEO U (n.d.), https://www.ideou.com/blogs /inspiration/what-is-design-thinking.

4. The Lean Startup (n.d.), http://theleanstartup.com/.

5. PBS, "The Television Program Transcripts: Part III: PBS Triumph of the Nerds," http://www.pbs.org/nerds/part3.html.

6. Rao, Sutton, and Webb, "Innovation Lessons from Pixar: An Interview with Brad Bird."

Chapter Twelve: Change Management and Company Culture: An Innovation Manifesto

1. Jay Greene, "10 Years Later, Amazon Celebrates Prime's Triumph," *The Seattle Times* (February 2, 2015), https://www.seattletimes.com/business/amazon/10-years-later-amazon-celebrates-primes-triumph.

2. Todd Spangler, "Amazon has more than 100 million Prime subscribers, Jeff Bezos discloses", *Variety* 18 April 2020, https://variety.com/2018/digital/news/ amazon-prime-100-million-subscribers-jeff-bezos-1202757832.

3. Gabriela Barkho, "Amazon's Q3 Earnings Show Company Invested Billions in Prime One-Day Delivery," *Observer* (October 25, 2019), https://observer.com/2019 /10/amazon-q3-earnings-prime-one-day-delivery-costs.

4. Mark Ellis, "Flush with Cash: British Airways Saves £600,000 on Fuel by Descaling Its Toilet Pipes," *The Mirror* (February 23, 2012), https://www.mirror.co.uk /news/uk-news/flush-with-cash-british-airways-saves-740383.

5. Goetz, "How 3M Gave Everyone Days Off and Created an Innovation Dynamo."

6. Eric von Hippel, *Free Innovation* (Cambridge: MIT Press, 2016), https:// evhippel.mit.edu.

7. von Hippel, *Free Innovation.*

8. von Hippel, *Free Innovation.*

9. Julia Milner and Trenton Milner, "Most Managers Don't Know How to Coach People: But They Can Learn," *Harvard Business Review* (August 14, 2018), https:// hbr.org/2018/08/most-managers-dont-know-how-to-coach-people-but-they-can-learn.

10. Lori Goler, Janelle Gale, Brynn Harrington, and Adam Grant, "Why People Really Quit Their Jobs," *Harvard Business Review* (January 11, 2018), https://hbr.org /2018/01/why-people-really-quit-their-jobs.

11. Ed Catmull, "How Pixar Fosters Collective Creativity," *Harvard Business Review* (September 2008), https://hbr.org/2008/09/how-pixar-fosters-collective-creativity.

12. Wolfgang Stroebe and Michael Diehl, "Why Groups Are Less Effective Than Their Members: On Productivity Losses in Idea-Generating Groups," *European Review of Social Psychology* vol. 5 (1994: 271-303), https://product.design.umn.edu/courses/pdes2701/documents/5701papers/04bluesky/streobe11.pdf.

Chapter Thirteen: How to Recognize and Use the Strengths of Incumbency

1. "Adieu AYEM!" AYEM (n.d.), https://www.myayem.co.uk.

2. Kevin White, "First Brand Launched by Danone Accelerator Scheme Rolls Out," *The Grocer* (November 15, 2018), https://www.thegrocer.co.uk/buying-and-supplying/new-product-development/first-brand-launched-by-danone-accelerator-scheme-rolls-out/573865.article.

3. Jules Scully, "Danone's Innovation Incubator Introduces Pati & Coco Desserts," *FoodbevMedia* (December 22, 2019), https://www.foodbev.com/news /danones-innovation-incubator-introduces-pati-coco-desserts.

4. Charlotte Rogers, "Alcoholic Kombucha and Salmon Skin Crisps: How Sainsbury's Innovation Team Chases 'Entrepreneurial Heat,'" *MarketingWeek* (June 24, 2019), https://www.marketingweek.com/sainsburys-future-brands-innovation.

5. Grand View Research, *Nutraceuticals Market Analyses by Product (Dietary Supplements, Functional Food, Functional Beverage), by Region (North America, Asia Pacific, Europe, CSA, MEA), and Segment Forecasts, 2018–2025* (San Francisco: Grand View Research, 2017), https://www.grandviewresearch.com/industry-analysis/nutraceuticals-market.

6. Capital requirements have been the bane of Tesla's existence and the primary reason the company is constantly raising money.

7. Catherine Clifford, "Coke CEO: Why We Have an Award for Projects That Fail," *CNBC Make It* (December 2, 2019), https://www.cnbc.com/2019/12/02/coke-ceo-quincey-why-coca-cola-co-has-award-for-projects-that-fail.html.

Chapter Fourteen:
From Dinosaurs to Eagles: Four Case Studies

1. *Apple iPad 2 Keynote, Special Event, March 2011,* YouTube, 1:08:43-1:09:09, https ://www.youtub e.com/watch?v=TGxEQhdhAQ.

2. Marshall B. Rosenberg, *Nonviolent Communication: A Language of Life,* 3rd ed. (Encinitas, California: PuddleDancer Press, 2015), https://www.amazon.com/Nonviolent-Communication-Language-Life-Changing-Relationships/dp/189200528X.

Chapter Fifteen:
Innovation Management Government

1. Henry Farrell, "This Year's Economics Nobel Winner Invented a Tool That's Both Brilliant and Undemocratic," *Vox* (October 16, 2018), https://www.vox.com/the-big-idea/2017/10/16/16481836/nudges-thaler-nobel-economics-prize-undemocratic-tool.

2. Richard H. Thaler and Cass R. Sunstein, *Nudge: Improving Decisions about Health, Wealth, and Happiness* (London: Penguin Books, 2008).

3. Michael Hallsworth, John A. List, Robert D. Metcalfe, and Ivo Vlaev, "The Behavioralist as Tax Collector: Using Natural Field Experiments to Enhance Tax Compliance," *Journal of Public Economics* 148 (127): 14-31, http://wrap.warwick.ac.uk/88777/1/WRAP-behavioralist-tax-collector-Vlaev-2017.pdf.

4. Anna Sallis, Hugo Harper, and Michael Sanders, "Effect of Persuasive Messages on National Health Service Organ Donor Registrations: A Pragmatic Quasi-Randomised Controlled Trial with One Million U.K. Road Taxpayers," *Trials* 19 (2018):513, https://www.ncbi.nlm.nih.gov/pmc/articles/PMC6150960.

5. Ben Quinn, "The 'Nudge Unit': The Experts That Became a Prime U.K. Export," *The Guardian* (November 11, 2018), https://www.theguardian.com/politics/2018/nov/10/nudge-unit-pushed-way-private-sector-behavioural-insights-team.

6. Nikhil R. Sahni, Maxwell Wessel, and Clayton M. Christensen, "Unleashing Breakthrough Innovation in Government," *Stanford Social Innovation Review* 2013 (summer): 27-31, https://ssir.org/articles/entry/unleashing_breakthrough _innovation_in_government.

7. Emily Files, "Laundromat Libraries Aim to Boost Literacy in Milwaukee," WUWM (October 10, 2019), https://www.wuwm.com/post/laundromat-libraries-aim-boost-literacy-milwaukee.

8. Joe Buchanan, "Monongalia County Health Department Uses Popular Dating App to Spread Health Alert," WDTV (November 21, 2019), https://www.wdtv.com/content/news/Monongalia-County-Health-Department-uses-popular-dating-app-to-spread-health-alert-565301431.html.

Conclusion: You Can't Ignore It; How Can You Embrace It?

1. Clayton M. Christensen, Michael E. Raynor, and Rory McDonald, "What Is Disruptive Innovation?" *Harvard Business Review* (December 2015), https://hbr.org /2015/12/what-is-disruptive-innovation.

2. Christensen, Raynor, and McDonald, "What Is Disruptive Innovation?"

INDEX

Accountability, lack of, 100-101
Agile methodology, 127
Agrawal, Ajay, 15
Air-quality sensors, 96-97
Akbar, Ali, 151
Alexa, 25, 41
Allbirds, 85
from zero to $1 billion in two years, 45-47
Amazon, 93, 122, 153, 183
Allbirds and, 46
ambidextrous leadership, 93-94
cloud service, 161, 163. *See also*
Amazon Web Services disruption and, 89-90
evolution, 44, 45
facilities, 43
vs. Google, 41, 90, 172 impact on retail commerce, 41
Innovator's Dilemma and, 49, 93
is remaking all of retail, 45
listening and, 94-96 vs.
Microsoft, 161, 163 Moore's law and, 37 most profitable parts of, 93 physical stores, 45 platforms and, 117-118
product searching on, 41-42
Sainsbury's and, xi, 183
small teams and, 122 and
subscriptions to products, 6
transportation and logistics, 32, 42. *See also* Amazon Prime
Amazon Alexa, 25, 41
Amazon Go, x, 44, 183
Amazon Prime, 186 birth of, 132-134 the lesson from, 134
Amazon Web Services, 112, 117-118. *See also* Amazon: cloud service
Ambidextrous leadership, 93-94
Andreessen, Marc, 70-71 203
Anheuser-Busch InBev (ABInBev), 148-150

Apple, 87, 130, 185
App Store, 113
    borrowing and copying, 129
    vs. Google, 62, 87
    innovation and, 89, 90, 130, 184-185
    vs. Microsoft, 160, 163
    Nike and, 97-98
    platforms and, 112-113
        practices, 116
    Steve Jobs and, 130, 155-156
    Xiaomi and, 72
Apple engineers, 62, 64
Apple Pay, 87, 186
Apple Watch, 10, 19, 36, 98, 185. *See also* iPhone Application programming interfaces (A.P.I.s), 114
Artificial intelligence (A.I.), 13
    ABInBev and, 166 advances in, 18, 197-198 information processing and, 129 medical devices and, 20 Netflix and, 54 and predictions, 15-16, 26 the scramble for, 16 Tesla and, 26, 48 TikTok and, 77 Watson and, 30
Assembly line, 52, 58 Asymmetric growth (platforms), 115
Automobiles. *See also Driver in the Driverless Car* as software and the art of the impossible, 47-49

Balance, struggle for, 104
Ballmer, Steve, 159, 160
Batteries, 48
Bedier, Osama, 86-87
Beeching, Philip, 95
Beinlich, Kurt, 136
Bell Labs, 58-59
Bezos, Jeff, 37, 133. *See also* Amazon
Bird, Brad, 99, 130
Black cabs, 14-15
Blank, Steve, 129
Blind (app), 82, 83
Bloomberg, Michael, 177
Boeing, 1-4
Borrowing liberally and literally, 129-130
Boston, 60-61
Brainstorming, 140-141
Brand, diminished influence of, 74-75
Britain. *See* Black cabs; Governments: British; Sainsbury's
British Airways, 121, 135, 138
Brynolfson, Erik, 52
Buyer, shift in power from seller to, 74
BuzzFeed, 38-39

Cable television, 36-38
    Netflix and, 36-38, 49
Cameras, 18, 44 digital, 28-29, 101 drones equipped with, 29, 166 Kodak and, 18, 28-29, 101 security, 155 smartphones and, 18, 25
Capital expenditures, large can be a weapon rather than a weakness, 148-149
Celebrated Failure Award, 151
    Chambers, John, 100. *See also*

Cultural transformation: *specific topics* failure to adapt and change, 89
Cheddar (TV channel), 39 China, 9, 68, 72, 77
Chips, computer, 6, 16
Christensen, Clayton M., 51, 53
disruption and, 32, 33, 97, 178, 184 on forming external businesses to compete with parent companies, 97 *Innovator's Dilemma,* 32-33, 97, 184 on requisites for public- sector innovation, 178 Tesla and, 49, 184, 185 Uber and, 38, 184, 185
Cisco
Eric Yuan at, 90-92 failure of, 90, 104
videoconferencing and, 89, 90
Cloud computing, 30, 37-38, 70. *See also* Amazon Web Services, 93 Microsoft and, 102, 159-160
Coaches, not bosses, 138-142 Coca-Cola, 151
Collaboration, 140-142
Comcast, 38
Common Threads initiative, 107, 109
Communication(s). *See also Nonviolent Communication* changes in style, substance, mechanism, and volume of communications, 81-82 DIY, cheap communications available to everyone, 78-79 how we communicate has changed everything, 76-79 unrestricted, free communications means loss of control, 79
Company culture. *See* Culture
Compensation packages, 67
Competition, 36, 45, 53, 65, 69, 184. *See also Regional Advantage;* Walmart; *specific topics* New Innovator's Dilemma and, 35, 36 platforms and, 115 against startups, ix, 7, 45, 51
Competitions, companywide, 121
Computer chips, 6, 16
Computing platforms. *See* Platforms COVID-19 (novel coronavirus disease 2019), 9, 10, 77, 167, 168
Cray supercomputers, 17
Crowdfunding, 128-129
Cruise Automation, 149 Cultural transformation, Microsoft's, 102, 158 changing culture, 161-163 move fast, fix things, be nicer, 159-161
Culture, 82, 132, 154. *See also under* Nadella, Satya; *specific topics* Eight Deadly Sins of Stasis and, 93 inappropriate, 101-103 of innovation, x, 56, 71, 138, 168, 187 of listening, 94 Silicon Valley and, 60, 71
Culture, people, and genuine connection, 60-61
Curtis, Alastair, 154 Customers, inability to solve real problems because of disconnection from real, 67-68

Danone, 144-145 and Ayem, 144-145 and Pati & Coco, 145
DARPA Grand Challenge, 125
Darrell, Bracken, 153-158
Defense Advanced Research Projects Administration (DARPA), 125
Delivery services/product delivery, 170. *See also* Amazon Prime food delivery, 114, 185 package delivery, 26-27
Design focus, 153
Design principles and purpose, 154-156
Design sprints, 126-128
Design thinking, 126-127
Design Thinking program, 141
DeWALT, 120-121 helps construction unplug, 120-121
Diffusion, innovation, 23 Diffusion of innovation model, 23, 23f
Disruption(s). *See also* Exponential disruption; *specific topics* Clayton Christensen and, 32, 33, 97, 178, 184 from first- to second-order, 24-26 massive media, 36-37 Tesla and, 184, 185
Distance, lack of, 97-98
Distribution power (platforms), 115
Diverse teams, 122
Diversifying, 156-157
Diversity, 63 and innovation, 34 of viewpoints, 140 Dollar Shave Club, 116, 156 came out of nowhere, 35 vs. Gillette, 5-6 innovation, 4, 5, 45 marketing, 5, 45, 173 razor blades and, 5-6 sales, 5 videos, 5 YouTube and, 5, 83
Dreamers, recruiting, 130-131
Driver in the Driverless Car: How Your Technology Choices Create the Future, The (Wadhwa and Salkever), 17, 20, key message, 20
Driverless cars, 48, 65, 75, 125
Drone delivery, 10, 26-27, 42
Drones, 26-27, 113, 125, 166

eBay, 35, 45, 109, 112, 113, 115
Ecosystems, innovation, 68 from marketplaces to platforms that support entire, 112 Silicon Valley, 61
Eight Deadly Sins of Stasis, 94-104
Electric-utility industry, 165
Empathy, 175. *See also Nonviolent Communication*
Employee suggestion box, digital, 132, 135, 138
Empowerment and experimentation, 142 checklist for, 142-143 Exponential disruption, 186. *See also specific topics* artificial intelligence (A.I.) and, 15. *See also* Artificial intelligence a case study in, 26-27 Exponential growth curves, 29 riding the curve, 163-165 Exponential innovation, what is driving, 17-19
Exponential technologies combining to become breakthrough innovations, 16-17

Exponentially advancing
technologies, ix, 18, 25-26, 53, 111, 156, 180. *See also specific topics*
Eyre, Rachel, 146

Facebook
copying others' products, 130 employees, 83, 154
platforms and, 2, 113, 115
Facebook advertising, 83, 150
Facilitation, 139
Factories, 52
battery, 48
drones and, 27
Failure, 151
Wall Street's lack of tolerance for, 89-90
Falcon Heavy, 1
FalconX, 1
Federal Aviation Authority (FAA), 26
Feedback (innovation game), 122
Feedback loops, 56, 178
Finance, 43-44
Fitbit, 19, 36, 97
Fitness trackers, 97. *See also* Fitbit
Food delivery, 114, 185
Ford Greenfield Labs, 64-65, 69
Ford Motor Company, 64-65, 69
FuelBand, 97-98
Future Brands, 145-147, 150

Gans, Joshua, 15
Gartner, 21, 22f
Gates, Bill, 159
General Electric (GE), 27, 117, 165
General Motors (GM), 49
Gerstner, Louis ("Lou"), 29, 102
Gigafactory, 48
Gillette, 5-6
Goldfarb, Avi, 15
Google, 36, 88, 127-128, 185, 186
vs. Amazon, 41, 159 vs. Apple, 62, 87-88 design sprints, 126-128 Design Thinking program, 141 driverless cars and, 65
Gmail, 77, 90, 134 high-speed Internet access and, 186
listening to employees for new ideas, 95
OKR (Objectives Key Results) model, 122
platforms and, 2, 112, 114-116
walkouts, 82, 83
Google AdWords, 5, 128, 166
Google Fi, 186
Google Maps, 14, 114
Google Pay, 86
Google Pay Send. *See* Google Wallet
Google Ventures, 87, 127
Google Wallet, what went wrong with, 86-88 inflexibility in its business model, 88 right product, right vision, wrong approach, 87
Government (technological) innovation challenges in innovation management, 174-176
expenditures and funding, 126, 176, 181
a golden age of, 180-181 nudges and, 178-180
requisites for, 192-195

Governments, 55, 59
British, 125, 175
Greeley, Greg, 133

Hall of Toast, 27, 28, 29, 30 and modern disruptors, 27-30
Hastings, Reed, 36-37, 39
Hewlett-Packard (HP), 28, 57, 97
HMV, 95-96
Holland, 62
Hulu, 37-39
Hype Cycle, 21-22, 22f

IBM, 29-30, 70, 93, 97, 102, 105
IBM Life Sciences, 29 Idea competitions, 121
Ideas, 170
listening to employees for new, 95
small innovation ideas can add up quickly, 134-135
IDEO, 76, 126-127
Incumbency, the many advantages of, 147-148
Incumbent superpowers, checklist of, 151
Industrial age, 52, 53
Industry 4.0, 18
Industry clusters, 56, 77 the failure of, 56-65, 71
Industry-academic partnerships, 56
Innovation. *See also specific topics*
creating innovation by reducing friction, removing barriers, 121-123
small innovation ideas can add up quickly, 134-135
Innovation black holes, 70
Innovation clusters, 64 *See also* Industry clusters
Innovation culture, x, 56, 71, 138, 168, 187, *See also specific topics*
Innovation Diffusion model, 23, 23f
Innovation friction, checklist for decreasing, 122-123
Innovation game, 33. *See also specific topics* ways it has changed, 33 Innovation manifesto and mindset for change, 135-137
Innovation platforms, 113, 114
Innovation prizes and contests, 124- 126
Innovator, checklist for making everyone an, 137
Innovator's Dilemma: When New Technologies Cause Great Firms to Fail, The (Christensen), 32-33, 97, 184. *See also* Christensen, Clayton M. Intellectual capital is "leakier" than ever, 75
iPhone, 18, 22, 130, 160

Jackets. *See under* Patagonia Jobs, Steve, 119, 130, 155

Kelly, Kevin, 80
Kinsa, 10
Knowledge, The, 13-15
Kodak, 18, 28-29, 101
Krishna, Arvind, 30

Launch, failure to, 89 Laundromats, mini-libraries in, 180

Lean startup methodologies, 142-143
Legacy brands, resource advantages of, 149-152
Legacy firms. *See also under* Open access, open source, and collective product development
lack of diversity and global perspective, 76
Libraries in laundromats, miniature, 180
Linux, 79, 172
Listening culture, 95
vs. unwillingness to listen, 94-96
Logitech
Bracken Darrell and, 153-158
design principles, 154
from slow death to thriving, 153-158
Longboard Island Lager, 150

Machine age, second, 52
Management, changes in, 34
Maps, 13-15, 114
Massachusetts Route 128 ("America's Technology Highway"), 60, 61
"Matrix management" system, 101
Maybury, Mark, 121
McAfee, Andrew, 52
Media companies, the fight for attention and shift in valuations of, 37-40
Media disruptions, massive, 36-37
Media services, over-the-top (OTT), 36, 38, 39, 49
Medical devices and technology, 9-10, 19. *See also* Fitness trackers
Merck, 58
Microsoft. *See also* Nadella, Satya vs. Amazon, 161
vs. Apple, 160, 163
reinvention of, 102. *See also* Cultural transformation,
Microsoft's smartphones and, 159, 162
Microsoft Azure, 159, 162-163
Money-transfer services, 44. *See also* Payment platform, Payment systems
Moore, Gordon, 57, 57f Moore's law, 17, 35, 37
Motivating, 138-139, 141
Mozilla, 96
Mozilla Connected Devices, 96
Musk, Elon, 1, 47-49

Nadella, Satya, 102
accomplishments, 102, 173 Amazon and, 161 background and overview, 159 boldness, 162 culture (change) and, 102, 103, 161-163 major moves, 162 move fast, fix things, be nicer, 159-161 *Nonviolent Communication* and, 159 on transformation, 103, 158
Net neutrality, 36
Netflix, 35-40, 49-50
Netherlands, 62
Network effects (platforms), 114
New Innovator's Dilemma, 32, 35

New Jersey, 58-59
NextEra Energy, x, 7 demonstrates innovation in a utility, 163
talent, consistency, and foresight, 164-165 a toe in the water, 165-166
Nike, 76, 97-98
Nokia, 101, 162
Nonviolent Communication (Rosenberg), 159
Noyce, Robert, 57, 57f
Nudge: Improving Decisions about Health, Wealth, and Happiness (Thaler and Sunstein), 174
Nudge unit, 174-175
Nudges, 174

Off the Eaten Path, 146 "1,000 True Fans" (Kelly), 80
Online commerce, 41-42. *See also* Amazon
Open access, open source, and collective product development, 79-82 changes in style, substance, mechanism, and volume of communications, 81-82
legacy communication channels are withering, 80-81
model of collaborative innovation, 80
Open-source operating system, 159 Open-source software community, 161
O'Reilly III, Charles A., 93, 94, 97
Organizational culture. *See* Culture Over-the-top (OTT) media services, 36, 38, 39, 49

Package delivery, 26-27. *See also* Delivery services/product delivery
Pandemics, 10
Parker, Geoffrey G., 117
Parking in Washington, DC, 178-179
ParkMobile, 179
Patagonia (clothing company), 110, 111, 116
Boulder store, 109-110
a business world turned upside down, 110
Common Threads initiative, 107, 109
consignment store, 110
Patagonia *(continued)*
"Don't Buy This Jacket" ad campaign, 107-112, 108f
eBay and, 109
revenue, 109, 110
Worn Wear program, 109-110
Patience, lack of, 97-97
Payment platform, mobile, 86-86, 113 switching to a, 179
Payment systems 43. *See also* Apple Pay
"People" people, recognizing, 158
Photography. *See also* Cameras digital, 28-29 film, 28-29
Pixar Animation Studios, 99, 100, 130, 131, 140
Platform characteristics, common, 114-115. *See also* Platforms asymmetric growth and competition, 115 distribution power, 115 network effects,

114 Platform design, innovative companies work hard on, 117
Platform-making company, programming Amazon to be a, 117-118
Platform Revolution (Parker et al.), 117
Platforms. *See also under* Ecosystems every company wants to be a platform company, 115-116 and marketplaces at the center of innovation breakthroughs, 116-117 transaction, innovation, and combined, 113-114
PM2.5 air quality sensor, 96
Political support, lack of, 103-104 Porter, Michael, 59-60, 64
Prediction machines, 15. *See also*
Artificial intelligence
Product development cycles moving faster, 75-76
Product searching, online, 41 Project SensorWeb, 96-97

Rahal, Peter, 84-85
Razor blades, 4-5. *See also* Dollar Shave Club
RCA (Radio Corporation of America), 27, 28, 58
Red Hat, 30, 161
Regional Advantage: Culture and Competition in Silicon Valley (Saxenian), 60
Research and development (R&D), 97 R&D centers, 65
Research and development (R&D) budgets, 56 and corporate performance, 56 reallocating R&D money, 158
Resources, lack of, 98 Ries, Eric, 129
Risks, failure to take, 89-90 Robo, Jim, 165
Robot vehicles, 125. *See also*
Driverless cars
Robots. *See also* Drones Amazon's use of, 19-20, 42-43
Rockets, 1. *See also* SpaceX Rogers, Everett, 23, 23f
Rosie (robotic maid), 19-20
Ross, Stephen, 82
Route 128. *See* Massachusetts Route 128
Rulebreakers, recruiting, 130-131
RXBAR, 84 from zero to $600 million in sales in five years, 84-85

Sainsbury's, 144-147, 183 Amazon and, xi, 183 cashierless technology and, xi Future Brands, 145-147, 150 Nectar loyalty program, 146
Salesforce, 112, 113, 161, 170
Salmon-skin crisps, 144
Saxenian, AnnaLee, 60
Sears, Roebuck and Company, 40
Second machine age, 52
Second-order innovator's dilemma, 49
Sensors, 20
advances in, 19
cheap, 17, 25, 181
medical, 19-20
PM2.5 air quality, 96

SensorWeb, 96-97
Shirky, Clay, 79
Silicon Valley, 55-56, 66-67, 72-73
advantages over competitors, x, 118
attempts to re-create/replicate, 58,
Boston compared with, 60-61
cooperation and sharing/ information exchange, 58, 61
culture and, 60, 71
ecosystem, 61 ethos, 66
Frederick Terman and, 58, 60
hiring Valley leaders and talent to staff outposts, 67
history and evolution, 60, 62, 64-65
innovation ecosystems and, 68
methods, 58, 130
origins and creation, 58, 59, 61
the power of an open system that welcomes outsiders, 61-64
problems, 68-69
stealing in, 144
Silicon Valley outposts, 64-65, 71, 100 boondoggles and junkets, 64-65
reasons for the failure of, 65-71
Silver, Spencer, 135
Simplifying, 156-157
Smartphone, 16, 96, 98, 114, 116. *See also* iPhone A.I. systems and, 19 cameras and, 18, 20, 25 cost savings resulting from, 78 flying, 114 impact, 13 Kodak and, 18, 29 limitations, 25
Microsoft and, 159, 162
Nokia and, 101-112, 162 PC peripherals and, 154
technologies incorporated into, 20, 24-25, 78
transportation and, 14, 38, 76, 193, 195
Xiaomi and, 72-73
Smith, Jared, 84-85
Social contagion, 23
Social networks, 74
Software, 77-78. *See also specific topics*
Software-as-a-Service (SaaS) business model, 163
SoulCycle, 81-82
SpaceX, 1-4, 49, 116, 186
Stanford University, 56-60, 64
Stanley Black & Decker, 120, 121
Startups, 32
competing against, 6, 7,
lean, 129
Steinberg, Jon, 39
Subscriptions, 5-6, 73. *See also* Amazon Prime; Dollar Shave Club; Netflix
Suggestion box, digital, 121, 135, 137, 138
Sunstein, Cass, 174
Survival as an endless task, 29-31

Tapscott, Don, 80
Taxes, 175
Teaching vs. telling, 139 Team size, 122
Teams, 69-71. *See also* Top- down corporate innovation teams
Technology. *See also specific topics*
the limits of, 19-20

Technology adoption curves, 24, 24f, 78
Technology shifts. *See also specific topics* are opening massive new markets, 76
Television, 80-81 cable, 36-40, 49
Terman, Frederick, 58-60
Tesla, 26, 35, 49, 113-114, 184
A.I., 26, 48
cars as software and the art of the impossible, 47-49
Clayton Christensen and, 49, 184, 185
disruption and, 184, 185
Model 3, 185
platforms and, 113-114
Thaler, Richard, 174-175
3M, 98, 126, 134-136, 138
"Toe in the water" strategy, 164-165, 166
Top-down corporate innovation teams, the folly of dedicated, 69
innovation black holes, 69-70
innovation teams can't see new business models, 70 innovation teams struggle to identify nascent markets, 70-71
Toyota, 94, 134, 138
Transaction platforms, 113
Transportation. *See also* Black cabs; Delivery services/product delivery;
Driver in the Driverless Car;
Drone delivery; Uber
smartphones and, 14, 38, 76, 193, 195
Trump, Donald J., 89 Trust, 36, 37
Trust systems, 37
Tushman, Mike L., 102, 103, 106-107

Uber, 13-15, 35, 184-185,
United Kingdom (UK). *See* Black cabs; Governments: British; Sainsbury's
Utility industry, 165

Venture capital, 60
spreading more broadly, 68
Venture-capital arms of companies,
69. *See also* Google Ventures
Venture capitalists, 61, 63 beer companies and, 164 Boston and, 60-61
capital investments, capital expenditures, and, 148-149
platform business and, 115
Videoconferencing Cisco and, 90, 91, 92
Eric Yuan and, 90, 92
Videoconferencing tools, 10, 91
Virtual reality (V.R.), 22-24, 157
Voice commerce and voice assistants, 41-42
von Behren, Rob, 87
von Hippel, Eric, 136

Wall, Jonathan, 87
Wall Street, lack of tolerance for failure, 89
Warby Parker, 45, 46
Ward, Charlie, 132

Watson (computer), 30
Webex, 91
Wikinomics: How Mass Collaboration Changes Everything (Williams), 80
Wikipedia, 80
Williams, Anthony D., 80
Windows Azure, 159, 160-161. *See also* Microsoft Azure
Worn Wear program, 109-110
    Wrong people and wrong role, 99-100

Xerox, 29, 89, 101
Xiaomi, 72-73
XPRIZE, 124-125

Yuan, Eric, 90-92, 98

Zoom (software), 77, 89, 90 Eric
    Yuan and, 90
Zoom Video Communications (Zoom), 77, 90, 98
    Cisco and, 89
Zuckerberg, Mark, 130, 186

ACKNOWLEDGEMENTS

My deepest debts of gratitude are always to my wonderful family, my reason for being. My younger son, Tarun, a natural scholar, deserves much credit for key ideas that appear in this book and that continue to show their worth in our exponential-innovation workshops. My elder son, Vineet; and my daughters-in-law, Ruhi and Neesha, have all provided incredible support to help me get back on my feet after the devastation of losing my dear wife, Tavinder.

I am proud to have co-authored the book with Ismail Amla. Ismail and I worked at my first startup, Seer Technologies, to help large companies develop advanced computer systems, and we have continued to work together throughout his career. Ours is a true learning partnership.

Both Ismail and I want to thank Alex Salkever for his work in putting words to the ideas and experiences that this book comprises. In 15 years of collaboration, Alex and I have co-authored three books and many articles. Alex combines his writing skills with an incredible understanding of technology and business; he is the best of the best. Our editor, John Harvey, is meticulous in his attention to detail in guiding our narrative and polishing our prose. As with all of the other books that I have authored and hundreds of columns for *The Washington Post*, *Fortune*, MarketWatch, *Hindustan Times*, and other publications, John played a crucial role as a trusted friend, adviser, and pain in the butt.

Lastly, we would all like to thank the people who rarely receive thanks: our book agent, Kathleen Anderson; and our publishers, Neal Maillett and Jeevan Sivasubramaniam. Sachin Sharma and his team at HarperCollins India for the Indian edition. All of them go out of their way to be helpful, and thereby help authors make an impact.

—Vivek Wadhwa

My contribution to this book is based on experience I have been lucky enough to accumulate over the past 30 years in working with the great leaders of some of the world's most iconic brands. I am deeply indebted to Keith Wilman, David Thomlinson, Lis Astall, Rob Heyvaert, Bridget van Kralingen, and Jon Lewis.

I am also very grateful to Vivek. He inspired me, pushed me, and coached me in writing this book. The Capita Institute's Dr. Oli Freestone, conducting important research in the world of work, was indispensable in providing feedback and ideas.

Lastly and perhaps more importantly: thanks to my friends and family for encouraging me to make the world a better place. Without your support and love, nothing would be possible.

—Ismail Amla

About the Authors

Vivek Wadhwa is a Distinguished Fellow at Harvard Law School's Labor and Worklife Program and a Distinguished Fellow and professor at Carnegie Mellon University's College of Engineering. He is the author of four best-selling books: *Your Happiness Was Hacked, The Driver in the Driverless Car, Innovating Women,* and *The Immigrant Exodus.*

He has been a globally syndicated columnist for *The Washington Post* and has held appointments at Duke University, Stanford Law School, Emory University, and Singularity University.

Wadhwa is based in Silicon Valley and researches, speaks, and writes about advancing technologies that are transforming our world. These advances—in fields such as robotics, artificial intelligence, computing, synthetic biology, 3D printing, medicine, and nanomaterials—are making it possible for small teams to do what was once possible only for governments and large corporations to do: solve the grand challenges in education, water, food, shelter, health, and security.

In 2012, the U.S. Government awarded Wadhwa distinguished recognition as an "Outstanding American by Choice" for his "commitment to this country and to the common civic values that unite us as Americans."

Alex Salkever is a writer, futurist, and technology leader. He is the co-author with Vivek Wadhwa of three books: *Your Happiness Was Hacked, The Driver in the Driverless Car,* and *The Immigrant Exodus.* A journalist both in print and on line, he has written dozens of articles exploring exponentially advancing technologies such as robotics, genomics, renewable energy, quantum computing, artificial intelligence, and driverless cars. He earlier served as the Technology Editor at BusinessWeek.com and as a guest researcher at the Duke University Pratt School of Engineering. He was most recently a Vice President at Mozilla. He speaks regularly at industry conferences, universities, and schools and to corporations and boards of directors. He lives in the Bay Area of California.

Ismail Amla is Chief Growth Officer at Capita, a £4 billion technology-services business based in the United Kingdom. Previously, he was Managing Partner for the $7 billion IBM Services business in North America, with responsibility for all industry sectors and a staff of more than 15,000.

In a career serving industries in all geographic regions, Amla has held executive positions with Fidelity Information Services, Capco, and Accenture.